The Invisible War

Building Business in the AI Era

Book Two of The Invisible War Series

By M.L. Ruscsak

Trient Press

The Invisible War: Building Business in the AI Era

This book is published by:

Trient Press®

1295 Grands Summit Dr, Suite B112

Reno, NV 89523

United States

Trient Press® is a registered trademark and legally owned company operating under the laws of the State of Nevada. All rights in the Trient Press® name, mark, and associated publishing identity are reserved.

ISBNs

Hardcover ISBN 979-8-88990-009-2

Paperback ISBN: 979-8-88990-072-6

E-book ISBN: 979-8-88990-070-2

First Edition

Printed in the United States of America.

The information contained in this book is provided for educational and informational purposes only. While every effort has been made to present accurate and practical business, AI, cybersecurity, and operational guidance, this book should not be interpreted as legal, financial, technical, or professional advice for any specific individual, business, or organization. Readers should consult qualified professionals for advice

Book design, publishing imprint, and related materials by Trient Press®.

Table of Contents

Foreword

By M.L. Ruscsak

There are moments in business when the ground does not simply shift. It accelerates. Owners feel it first in small ways: the customer who expects an answer before lunch, the invoice that should have been automatic, the team member who is buried in repetitive work, the tool that promised simplicity but created one more place to check. Then the pressure becomes impossible to ignore. The business is still standing, but the pace around it has changed.

That is the world this book steps into. The Invisible War: Building Business in the AI Era is not written for people who want to sound impressive at conferences. It is written for the leader who has to make payroll, protect customer trust, answer the phone, keep the team moving, and still find time to understand what artificial intelligence is going to change. It is written for people who do not have the luxury of waiting until the future becomes convenient.

The strength of this book is that it does not treat AI like a magic trick. It does not ask the reader to abandon common sense or pretend that every new tool deserves applause. Instead, it brings the conversation back to business fundamentals: clarity, trust, judgment, accountability, security, speed, and service. Those words may sound familiar, even old-fashioned, but in the AI era they become more important, not less. Technology can move faster than people. It cannot care more than people. It cannot take responsibility for the business owner. It cannot replace the discipline of knowing what matters and protecting it.

M.L. writes from the place where modern pressure actually lives. Not from a distant theory. Not from hype. Not from fear. The voice in these pages is warm enough to make the reader feel seen and firm enough to tell the truth. That combination matters. Many business owners already feel behind, and the last thing they need is another expert making them feel small. What they need is a translator. They need someone who can take a complicated shift and say, in plain language, here is what changed, here is why it matters, and here is how you begin to respond without losing yourself in the process.

One of the most important ideas in this book is that AI is not simply another tool on the desk. It is becoming an operating layer. That may sound technical at first, but the meaning is practical. AI is starting to touch decisions, workflows, customer experiences, financial visibility, security posture, hiring, service, marketing, and leadership. When something touches that much of the business, it cannot be managed casually. It needs structure. It needs boundaries. It needs a human being who is still in charge.

This book is also a needed correction to the extremes of the current conversation. On one side are the people who say AI will solve everything. On the other side are the people who hope ignoring it will make the problem disappear. Both positions are dangerous. The businesses that survive and grow will be the ones that can move faster without becoming reckless, automate work without surrendering judgment, and adopt new systems without sacrificing trust. That is not a technology problem alone. It is a leadership problem.

For the average business owner, this may be the most reassuring message in the book: you do not need to become a machine to compete in a machine-speed world. You need to become more disciplined about how your business thinks, decides, protects, and improves. You need a clearer control room. You need cleaner information. You need better guardrails. You need to know what should be automated and what should never leave human hands. The future will reward leaders who can make that distinction.

The Invisible War is a fitting title because the most important battles in business are not always visible from the outside. They happen inside the systems, inside the habits, inside the delays, inside the trust gaps, inside the handoffs no one owns. By the time the market sees the difference, the stronger business has already built the operating discipline behind the scenes. This book gives readers language for that hidden work and a way to begin building it.

Read this book with a pen nearby. Not because it is difficult, but because it will make you think about your business differently. You will recognize places where speed is exposing old weakness. You will see where scattered tools have been mistaken for strategy. You will understand why security and operations now belong in the same conversation. Most of all, you will feel the invitation underneath the warning: the AI era does not have to belong only to giant companies with giant budgets. It can belong to disciplined leaders who are willing to build differently.

That is the promise of these pages. Not panic. Not perfection. Preparedness. And in the era ahead, preparedness may be the most valuable advantage a business can own.

Introduction

There is a particular kind of tired that only business owners understand. It is not just physical tired. It is not even just mental tired. It is the feeling of opening your laptop in the morning and realizing the business has already started without you. The inbox is full. The messages are stacked. The calendar has moved. The customer who was patient yesterday wants an answer today. The software sent an alert. The bank account needs attention. The team needs direction. The social platforms want content. The systems want passwords. Somewhere in the middle of all of that, someone is telling you that artificial intelligence is going to change everything and you need to hurry up.

That is not a strategy. That is pressure with better marketing.

This book begins with a simple truth: most people are not behind because they are not smart. They are behind because business changed shape faster than the average person was given language to understand it. The old model of business was demanding, but it was easier to picture. You had customers, employees, paperwork, products, services, vendors, bills, and a reputation to protect. It was never easy, but at least the boundaries were more visible. Today, the business is not only what happens in the building, on the website, or inside the books. It is also what happens across platforms, automations, algorithms, cloud systems, payment tools, customer data, search results, security alerts, and now

AI models that can produce answers faster than a team can schedule a meeting.

That is why AI cannot be treated like a shiny gadget. It is not just something you add to your business when you have extra time. It is becoming part of the way business moves. It changes how quickly work can be produced, how customers expect to be served, how competitors make decisions, how employees handle repetitive tasks, how owners see information, and how mistakes spread when no one is paying attention. Used well, AI can give a business clarity, leverage, and speed. Used carelessly, it can make confusion look productive.

I want to say that again because it may be one of the most important lines in this book: AI can make confusion look productive. A disorganized business with AI does not automatically become modern. It often becomes a faster mess. A company with unclear rules can automate the wrong behavior. A team with messy data can create polished nonsense. An owner without visibility can buy more tools and still have less control. The promise of AI is real, but it does not remove the need for leadership. It exposes the quality of leadership faster.

That is the invisible war this book is about. It is not a war against machines. It is not a war against progress. It is the hidden struggle between businesses that learn to operate with discipline in the AI era and businesses that keep reacting until reaction becomes their entire operating model. It is the fight for trust, clarity, speed, judgment, security, and control in a world that rewards movement but punishes carelessness.

I wrote this book for the person who hears the word AI and feels two things at the same time: curiosity and exhaustion. You may understand that something important is happening, but still wonder where to begin. You may have tried tools that looked impressive for a week and then quietly became one more login. You may have employees using AI without clear rules, vendors promising miracles, competitors moving faster, or customers expecting service that feels instant and personal. You may be excited. You may be skeptical. You may be both before breakfast. That is allowed here.

This will not be a book that shames you for not knowing everything. It will not bury you in technical language just to prove the subject is complicated. It will not tell you to fire your team, replace your judgment, or hand your business to a machine. I do not believe that is leadership. I believe leadership in the AI era means learning how to combine human judgment with machine speed without letting either one become dangerous. It means knowing what to automate and what to protect. It means building systems that make the business easier to see, not harder to understand.

When I talk about building business in the AI era, I am not talking about chasing every new app that appears on your screen. Tool-hopping is not transformation. Downloading software is not the same as becoming operationally stronger. The real question is not, What AI tool should I buy? The better question is, What kind of business am I building, and where does intelligence need to live inside it? That question changes everything. It moves the conversation from novelty to design. It forces us to look at the business as a living system with signals, decisions, risks, people, promises, and proof.

Every business already has an operating system, whether the owner has named it or not. It is the way information moves. It is the way decisions get made. It is the way customers are followed up with or forgotten. It is the way money is tracked, files are stored, approvals are handled, and mistakes are discovered. In some businesses, that operating system is clear and intentional. In many others, it is a patchwork of memory, habit, spreadsheets, messages, and heroic last-minute effort. AI does not erase that reality. It plugs into it. If the system underneath is strong, AI can strengthen it. If the system underneath is chaotic, AI can multiply the chaos.

This is where many leaders get misled. They are told the future belongs to whoever adopts AI first. I do not think that is the full truth. The future belongs to the businesses that can adopt AI with discipline. Speed matters. But speed without trust becomes chaos. Trust matters. But trust without speed becomes stagnation. The modern business has to learn how to carry both. It has to move quickly enough to compete and carefully enough to remain credible.

That balance is especially important because AI is arriving at the same time business risk is becoming more connected. A customer service mistake can become a reputation problem. A data mistake can become a legal problem. A workflow mistake can become a financial problem. A security mistake can become an existential problem. The old habit of treating operations, technology, finance, customer experience, and security as separate rooms no longer works as well. In the AI era, those rooms share walls. What happens in one part of the business can create consequences in another before anyone has time to call a meeting.

That is why I often think in terms of a control room. Not a cold, intimidating command center reserved for massive corporations, but a clear place where the owner can see what matters. A control room means the business has visibility. It means important signals are not buried. It means someone knows what the systems are doing. It means decisions have context. It means automation has guardrails. It means the business can move without becoming blind. Every business needs some version of that now, even if it starts very simple.

The good news is that becoming AI-ready does not require you to become someone else. You do not need to lose your personality, your common sense, your customer care, or your human way of leading. In fact, those things may become more valuable. As machines produce more content, customers will look harder for proof. As automation becomes cheaper, trust will become more expensive. As competitors move faster, the businesses that can explain themselves clearly and serve people reliably will stand out. The human part of business is not disappearing. It is being tested.

Throughout this book, we are going to talk plainly about what changed, how the system works now, where the threats are, what a survival framework looks like, and how leaders can prepare for the future without becoming overwhelmed by it. We will talk about AI as an operating layer, not a party trick. We will talk about data, decisions, customer journeys, fragmented tools, cybersecurity, automation, team roles, and trust. We will talk about what should move faster and what should never be rushed. Most importantly, we will keep bringing the conversation back to real business life, because that is where the pressure is felt and where the solutions have to work.

If you are reading this as a business owner, founder, manager, creator, consultant, executive, or professional trying to understand where you fit in this new era, I want you to know this: you are not late beyond repair. You are standing in a transition. Transitions are uncomfortable because the old map stops matching the road. That does not mean you are lost. It means you need a better map.

This book is that map. It will not do the work for you. No book can. But it will help you see the work differently. It will give you language for decisions you already feel but have not been able to name. It will help you recognize the difference between useful automation and expensive distraction. It will show why security is no longer a separate technical conversation but part of business trust. It will help you build a stronger rhythm for operating in a world that will not slow down just because people are tired.

The AI era is not waiting for perfect conditions. It is already here, inside the tools people use, the expectations customers bring, the speed competitors chase, and the risks leaders must manage. The question is not whether business will change. It already has. The question is whether you will build a business that can see clearly, decide wisely, move quickly, and protect trust while everything around it accelerates.

That is the work ahead. And it is work worth doing.

Part One - What Changed

Part One - What Changed

Chapter 1
The Day Business Got Faster Than People

There is a moment every modern business owner knows, even if they have never named it. You open your laptop or pick up your phone, and before you have had a full thought of your own, the business is already talking at you. There is an email from a customer who expected an answer yesterday. A message from a vendor asking for a decision. A bank alert. A software update. A social media notification. A calendar reminder. A security warning you are not sure is serious, but you are also not comfortable ignoring. Before the day has even properly begun, you are not leading the business. You are reacting to it.

That feeling is not laziness. It is not a character flaw. It is not proof that you are bad at business. It is proof that the speed of business has changed faster than the average operating system inside most companies. And by operating system, I do not mean a computer program. I mean the way a business thinks, moves, decides, communicates, follows up, protects itself, and knows what is true.

For a long time, business moved at a human pace. A customer called. You called back. A proposal was drafted. Someone reviewed it. The team met. The next step happened. There were always busy seasons, emergencies, and demanding clients, but the rhythm was still recognizable.

People could catch up because the systems around them waited. The phone rang, then it stopped. The mailbox filled, then it was sorted. The meeting ended, and everyone had at least a little space before the next wave arrived.

That world did not disappear all at once. It faded. Then, almost overnight, it felt gone.

Now the business does not wait. Customers compare you while standing in line at the grocery store. Competitors publish, advertise, follow up, and adjust while you are still thinking through the last campaign. Software sends reminders before people do. Platforms grade your response time. Algorithms reward consistency whether or not your team has the bandwidth to be consistent. Cyber threats do not care that you are short staffed. And AI has entered the room not as a polite assistant waiting patiently in the corner, but as an acceleration layer sitting on top of nearly everything.

That is the day business got faster than people. Not because people became less capable, but because the environment around them changed speed.

The new speed of normal

One of the hardest parts of this era is that the pressure often looks ordinary from the outside. A business can look fine. The logo is fine. The website is fine. The owner is smart. The team is trying. The customers are still there. Nothing dramatic has exploded. But inside, everything feels louder. More decisions are arriving than the old system was built to handle. More information is being created than anyone has time to organize. More tools are being added because every tool promises to save time, yet somehow the owner has less time than before.

This is why so many people feel behind even while working harder than ever. They are not behind in effort. They are behind in structure. The old structure assumed that a person could hold the business together by memory, instinct, personality, and persistence. That worked when the business was smaller, the channels were fewer, and the pace was slower. But in the AI era, memory is too fragile, instinct is too delayed, personality is not a process, and persistence by itself can turn into exhaustion.

I have seen this in real business conversations over and over again. The owner does not usually say, "My operating model has failed to adapt to machine-speed expectations." That would be a very formal way to describe a very human problem. What they say is, "I am tired." They say, "I know I need to use AI, but I do not know where to start." They say, "I have too many tools." They say, "I feel like I am always missing something." They say, "I cannot keep doing everything this way."

Those sentences matter. They are the human language of a business system under strain.

And here is where the conversation about AI can become dangerous. When people are already overwhelmed, the market often hands them another tool and calls it transformation. It says, "Use this to write faster. Use this to sell faster. Use this to automate your team. Use this to create content. Use this to answer customers. Use this to replace the boring work." Some of those tools may be useful. Some may be excellent. But a tool added to confusion does not automatically create clarity. Sometimes it only makes the confusion move faster.

That is one of the most important truths in this book: AI does not fix disorder. It accelerates whatever is already there.

If your follow-up process is strong, AI may help it move with more consistency. If your customer data is clean, AI may help you see patterns faster. If your team knows who is responsible for what, AI may reduce repetitive work. But if your information is scattered, your roles are unclear, your customer promises are inconsistent, and nobody knows which system is the source of truth, AI can make the business feel modern while the foundation is still cracking underneath it.

When speed exposes the system

A faster business environment is not automatically a better one. Speed is only helpful when it is connected to direction. A car going eighty miles an hour in the wrong lane is not more advanced than a car going forty in the right one. It is just more dangerous. Business works the same way. Faster marketing, faster decisions, faster customer responses, and faster automation only help when the company knows what it is trying to protect and where it is trying to go.

This is why the first chapter of this book does not begin with a technical definition of artificial intelligence. We will get to the practical side. We will talk about systems, judgment, automation, data, security, workflows, and leadership. But before we do any of that, we have to name the feeling. Because if we do not name the feeling, business owners will keep reaching for tools as emotional relief instead of building systems as strategic protection.

The feeling is this: the business is moving faster than the person responsible for it can comfortably process.

That does not mean the person is weak. It means the business has entered a different kind of weather. If you walked outside in a light jacket and a storm arrived, you would not stand there shaming yourself for being cold. You would say, "The conditions changed. I need different protection." That is the right way to think about the AI era. The conditions changed. The tools changed. The expectations changed. The threats changed. The tempo changed. So the way we build and run a business has to change with it.

I often think about this through the lens of building a security-first business operating platform. When you are building something like that, you cannot afford to believe that scattered information will somehow organize itself later. You cannot afford to treat trust as a nice extra. You cannot afford to let every tool make its own version of the truth. You learn very quickly that speed without structure is not innovation. It is risk wearing a better outfit.

That lesson applies far beyond technology companies. It applies to the bakery trying to manage orders, payroll, reviews, and delivery apps. It applies to the consultant juggling proposals, invoices, client notes, and follow-up. It applies to the construction company tracking crews, materials, permits, photos, expenses, and customer updates. It applies to the creator trying to turn attention into a real business without losing their mind. It applies to the local service company whose entire reputation can be affected by one unanswered message, one billing mistake, or one security incident.

The AI era did not only change the tools available to the Fortune 500. It changed the expectations placed on everybody else.

The mistake is trying to outrun the machine

When business starts moving at machine speed, the natural human instinct is to try to work faster. Wake up earlier. Answer more messages. Subscribe to another app. Push the team harder. Watch more tutorials. Copy what competitors are doing. Fill the calendar. Keep the laptop open later. Tell yourself you will organize everything once things calm down.

But things do not calm down by themselves. Not in this era. The stream keeps streaming. The inbox keeps filling. The customer keeps expecting. The threat landscape keeps shifting. The software keeps updating. The marketplace keeps rewarding whoever can show up with more relevance, more consistency, more trust, and less friction.

Trying to outrun the machine is a losing strategy because the machine does not get tired. That sentence can sound intimidating, but it is also freeing. You do not have to become a machine. You should not become one. The goal is not to erase your humanity, your judgment, your values, or your relationships. The goal is to stop forcing your human mind to do work that a disciplined system should be helping you carry.

There is a big difference between leadership and mental clutter. Leadership is deciding what matters. Mental clutter is trying to remember every loose end. Leadership is setting standards. Mental clutter is checking five places to figure out whether the customer was called. Leadership is reading the situation and making a judgment. Mental clutter is digging through old emails to reconstruct the basic facts. Leadership belongs to the human. Clutter should be removed from the human as much as possible.

This is where AI becomes useful, but only if we put it in the right place. AI should not be treated as a magic personality that rescues a disorganized business from the consequences of being disorganized. AI should be treated as part of an operating layer that helps information move, patterns surface, repetitive work shrink, and decisions become more visible. The human still leads. The system supports. The business becomes faster because it becomes clearer, not because everyone is panicking at a higher speed.

That distinction matters because many leaders are being sold an emotional fantasy. The fantasy says, "Buy the right AI tool and the business will become easy." I do not believe that is true. AI can make parts of business easier. It can make certain tasks dramatically faster. It can help draft, sort, summarize, compare, monitor, remind, and recommend. But it cannot care about your reputation the way you do. It cannot understand the full weight of a promise unless you have built a system that defines the promise. It cannot protect trust if the business itself has not decided what trust requires.

The businesses that win in this era will not simply be the ones that use AI. They will be the ones that use AI inside a disciplined human-led structure. They will know what should be automated, what should be assisted, what should be reviewed, and what should never be handed over without human judgment. They will not confuse speed with wisdom. They will not confuse activity with progress. They will not confuse a tool subscription with a strategy.

That is a different kind of leadership. It is calmer. It is clearer. It is not less ambitious. It is more controlled.

What changed inside the customer

We also have to be honest about the customer. The customer changed too. Not because customers became bad people, but because their environment trained them to expect more. They are used to instant confirmations, live tracking, personalized recommendations, searchable answers, automated reminders, and quick comparison. They may still love human service, but their tolerance for confusion has gone down.

A customer may not care whether your business uses AI. They care whether you remember what they asked for. They care whether the invoice makes sense. They care whether the appointment is confirmed. They care whether the answer is timely. They care whether their data is protected. They care whether your business feels steady or scattered. AI is often invisible to them, but the results are not.

That is part of the invisible war. Much of the competition is no longer happening only in the obvious places. It is not only who has the prettiest storefront, the loudest advertisement, or the biggest sales pitch. It is happening in response time, clarity, follow-through, proof, security, personalization, and operational trust. It is happening in the small moments where a customer decides whether you feel reliable.

Reliability used to be mostly a character trait. Now it also has to be a system trait. You can be a deeply reliable person and still run a business that accidentally feels unreliable because the information is scattered. You can care about your customers and still miss details because your process depends on memory. You can be honest and still create confusion because your tools are disconnected. In the AI era, good intentions need better infrastructure.

This is where a business starts to shift from reacting to operating. Reacting asks, "What is on fire today?" Operating asks, "What do we need to see every week so fewer things catch fire?" Reacting asks, "Which tool can solve this one pain point?" Operating asks, "How should information move through the business so the right person sees the right thing at the right time?" Reacting asks, "How do I catch up?" Operating asks, "What system keeps us from falling behind in the same way again?"

That shift is the beginning of maturity in the AI era. It is not glamorous at first. It does not always look like a viral breakthrough. It looks like knowing where customer information lives. It looks like having a real follow-up rhythm. It looks like using AI to summarize the right inputs instead of guessing from scattered scraps. It looks like reviewing automated work before it touches the customer. It looks like protecting passwords, access, records, and reputation with the same seriousness you bring to sales.

The business control room

As we move through this book, I am going to come back to the idea of a control room. Not a cold, complicated room with giant screens and people barking commands. I mean a simple business idea: the owner or leader should be able to see what matters, know what changed, understand what needs attention, and make better decisions without digging through chaos.

Every business needs some version of that now. A control room may be advanced software for one company and a very disciplined dashboard plus weekly rhythm for another. The point is not the fanciness of the technology. The point is visibility. If you cannot see what is happening, you cannot lead it. If you cannot tell which information is true, you cannot trust it. If you cannot trust it, you cannot automate around it safely. And if you cannot automate safely, the AI era becomes a stress multiplier instead of an advantage.

A control room mindset changes the question. Instead of asking, "What AI tool should I try?" you begin asking, "What part of my business needs better visibility, better speed, better protection, or better follow-through?" That question is much more powerful because it starts with the business, not the software. It makes AI serve the operation instead of letting the operation chase AI.

Those are AI-era questions. They are also leadership questions. That is the heart of this book. The future of business will not belong only to people who can code, prompt, automate, or analyze data. It will belong to people who can combine technology with judgment. People who can move faster without becoming careless. People who can use systems without becoming servants to systems. People who can protect trust while increasing speed.

That is why I do not want this book to make you feel small. I want it to make the moment feel understandable. You are not behind because you lack intelligence. You may be behind because the old way of running the business was built for a slower world. Once you see that, shame loses power. The question is no longer, "What is wrong with me?" The question becomes, "What does my business need now that the world moves this way?"

That question is where leadership begins again.

The first shift

The first shift is mental. Before you buy more technology, before you automate another task, before you feel pressured to become an AI expert, you have to accept that business has entered a different speed class. That does not mean every old principle is dead. Trust still matters. Cash flow still matters. Customers still matter. Quality still matters. Leadership still matters. In fact, those things matter more because the consequences of weakness show up faster.

A poor customer experience can spread faster. A sloppy process can repeat faster. A confusing message can reach more people faster. A bad assumption can be copied into more decisions faster. A security mistake can travel through more systems faster. That is why the AI era requires both ambition and discipline. You need the courage to use new capability, and you need the maturity to put guardrails around it.

This is not a call to slow down and hide from the future. It is a call to stop confusing uncontrolled speed with progress. The answer to machine-speed business is not human panic. The answer is human-led systems. The answer is clarity. The answer is trust architecture. The answer is a business that knows what it knows, protects what it must protect, automates what should be automated, and keeps human judgment where human judgment belongs.

That may sound like a high standard. It is. But it is also reachable. You do not build it in one dramatic weekend. You build it by seeing the business differently. You build it by choosing one area at a time and asking better questions. You build it by refusing to let technology become a costume for chaos. You build it by deciding that the business is not going to be dragged into the AI era by fear, hype, or exhaustion. It is going to be led there with purpose.

The day business got faster than people was not the end of human leadership. It was the end of pretending that human leadership could keep carrying everything manually. That is an important distinction. The future does not ask you to become less human. It asks you to stop using human energy on work that should be organized, supported, and protected by better systems.

This book is going to help you build both. We will look at what changed, how AI functions as an operating layer, where the traps live, how to protect judgment, how to design a secure stack, how to lead a team through change, and how to compete against businesses that move faster than yours. But it starts here, with the simplest truth: business did not just get busier. It got faster.

And once business gets faster than people, the winning move is not to become a machine. The winning move is to build a business that lets people lead at the speed the moment requires.

AI does not replace leadership. It exposes whether the business has enough structure for leadership to move at modern speed.

Part One - What Changed

Chapter 2

The End of the Old Workday

For a long time, the workday had a shape. It may not have been perfect. It may not have been easy. But most people could still recognize its edges. There was a beginning, a middle, and an end. You arrived, opened the store, unlocked the office, turned on the computer, checked the messages, did the work, handled the customers, closed the register, shut the door, drove home, and at least in theory, the day was done.

Of course, business owners have always worked more than the neat little version of the workday suggests. Anybody who has ever run payroll at midnight, answered a customer on a Sunday, or worried about cash flow while making dinner knows that ownership has never fit cleanly inside office hours. But even then, there was a difference between being busy and being constantly reachable. There was a difference between work following you home and work living in your pocket.

That difference matters because the old workday did not end with a dramatic announcement. Nobody sent a memo saying, 'Starting Monday, your business will no longer respect time, attention, sleep, family dinner, weekends, or mental space.' It just happened. A little more email. A little more texting. A few more apps. Customers expecting faster answers. Platforms sending alerts. Employees needing decisions in new channels. Vendors using portals. Banks using dashboards. Software asking to be updated. Social media demanding consistency. Then AI arrived and added another layer of speed on top of the whole thing.

Suddenly the workday was not a day anymore. It became a stream.

That is one of the biggest changes leaders have to understand in the AI era. We are not only changing tools. We are changing time. We are changing the rhythm of decisions, the pace of communication, the way information enters the business, and the amount of mental sorting expected from one person. The old workday was built around tasks. The new workday is built around signals. Something is always pinging, updating, requesting, warning, reminding, recommending, or asking to be approved.

If Chapter 1 was about business getting faster than people, Chapter 2 is about where that speed lands first: inside the day itself.

The workday used to have walls

The old workday had walls. Not always strong walls, but walls. The phone had a place. Files had a cabinet. Customers had business hours. Meetings happened in rooms. Mail arrived once a day. The pace of information was limited by the physical world. Even when things were stressful, there were natural pauses built into the system.

Those pauses did more than give people a break. They gave leaders time to think. A customer request might wait until the next morning. A vendor question might sit until the next scheduled call. A financial report might come once a month. A marketing campaign might take weeks to evaluate. That rhythm had problems, but it also had breathing room. Business could be slower than ideal, but the slowness sometimes protected judgment.

Today, that breathing room is easy to lose. A customer can message through the website, social media, email, text, a review platform, or a scheduling system. An employee can reach you through chat, email, phone, project software, or a shared document. A payment can fail while you are in the grocery store. A security alert can arrive while you are getting ready for bed. AI can draft a proposal in seconds, but then someone still has to decide if the proposal is right, safe, accurate, on-brand, and worth sending.

That is the part people miss. Faster production does not automatically create more leadership capacity. Sometimes it creates more things to review. More output can become more obligation. More communication can become more noise. More options can create more decisions. When the walls around the workday disappear, the leader does not simply gain flexibility. The leader inherits a stream that never fully shuts off.

That is the end of the old workday. Not because people stopped working. Because work stopped staying where we put it.

The stream is not the same as the work

One of the most important distinctions in modern business is the difference between the work and the stream. The work is what actually moves the business forward. Serving the customer. Making the product better. Reviewing the numbers. Training the team. Protecting sensitive information. Building relationships. Improving the offer. Keeping promises. The stream is everything that flows toward you while you are trying to do those things.

Without a sorting system, everything starts to feel equally urgent. The discount code, the angry customer, the low-risk notification, the high-risk security warning, the missed invoice, the staff question, the calendar reminder, the new AI feature, the marketing idea, and the personal text message all arrive through the same nervous system. The owner becomes the filter. The owner becomes the router. The owner becomes the dashboard. And that is too much weight for one human brain to carry all day.

This is where a lot of people misunderstand productivity. They think the problem is that they need to become better at answering everything. But answering everything is not the same as leading. Sometimes the more powerful move is to decide what should reach you, when it should reach you, who should handle it first, and what information must be visible before a decision is made.

That may sound simple, but it is a major leadership shift. In the old workday, time itself created some of that order. Doors opened and closed. Calls came through certain lines. Paper sat in physical stacks. People could see where the work was. In the AI era, the work is often invisible until it becomes a problem. It lives in dashboards, inboxes, automations, permissions, documents, databases, and third-party systems. If nobody designs the flow, the flow designs the day for you.

And if the flow designs the day, the business may look active while the leader is quietly losing control.

Attention became a business asset

In the old model, leaders talked about time management. In the new model, we have to talk about attention management. Time is still important, of course. You only get so many hours in a day. But attention is the part of time that can actually make a decision, notice a risk, hear what a customer is really saying, or recognize when a team member is overwhelmed.

A full calendar is not the same as a focused business. A fast inbox is not the same as a smart operation. A leader can spend twelve hours responding and still never reach the work that changes the future. That is why attention has become one of the most valuable assets in a modern company. Wherever the leader's attention goes, energy follows. Wherever attention is stolen, the business pays a hidden tax.

AI can help with that, but only if we understand the problem correctly. AI can summarize, draft, sort, classify, remind, compare, and surface patterns. That can be incredibly helpful. But AI can also create more content, more suggestions, more notifications, more options, and more decisions. Used poorly, it becomes a fire hose attached to another fire hose. Used well, it becomes part of the filtering system that protects human attention for the work that actually needs human judgment.

Think about a customer complaint. AI may help summarize the history, pull the invoice, find the last message, and draft a response. That is useful. But the judgment of what tone to use, when to call instead of email, whether the customer has a deeper frustration, and what the business should learn from the situation still belongs to leadership.

The tool can reduce the clutter around the decision. It should not replace the care inside the decision.

When attention becomes a business asset, protecting it is not selfish. It is responsible. A leader who is mentally scattered cannot protect trust as well as a leader who can see clearly. A team that is constantly interrupted cannot produce thoughtful work. A business that treats every signal as urgent will eventually miss the signal that actually matters.

The new workday is a rhythm, not a schedule

The answer is not to pretend we can return to the old workday exactly as it was. That would be comforting, but it would not be honest. Customers are not going to unlearn speed. Software is not going to stop connecting. AI is not going to politely step out of the economy because we feel overwhelmed. The world has moved. The question is whether we can build a better rhythm inside the movement.

A schedule tells you where to be. A rhythm tells the business how to breathe. That is the shift. In an AI-era company, the leader needs more than a calendar. The business needs a rhythm for reviewing what happened, deciding what matters, protecting sensitive decisions, and moving repetitive work out of the human bottleneck without losing accountability.

That rhythm does not have to be complicated. In fact, the best version is usually surprisingly plain. The business needs a regular time to look at money, customers, team capacity, operational risk, security, marketing, and follow-through. It needs a way to know which information is trusted. It needs a way to separate routine work from judgment work. It needs a way to make sure automation is helping the mission instead of quietly creating new messes.

This is where the idea of a business control room begins to matter again. A control room is not only a dashboard. It is a rhythm of seeing. What do we check every morning? What do we review every week? What should never be automated without approval? Which alerts deserve immediate attention? Which updates can wait? Which numbers tell the truth? Which customer patterns are trying to teach us something?

The old workday asked, 'What do I have to do today?' The new workday asks, 'What does the business need to know, decide, protect, and improve today?' That may sound like a small difference. It is not. One question creates a task list. The other creates leadership.

AI did not erase the human day

There is a fear underneath many conversations about AI that people do not always say out loud. The fear is that if work gets faster, people will be expected to become less human. Less tired. Less distracted. Less emotional. Less in need of pauses. Less in need of family, rest, reflection, and quiet. The fear is that the machine-speed business world will treat human limits as a defect.

I understand that fear. But I do not think the answer is to surrender to it. The answer is to build businesses that use AI to protect the human day, not destroy it. That is a very different intention. If AI is only used to produce more, demand more, push more, and squeeze more, then it becomes another pressure system. But if AI is used to remove repetitive drag, surface important information, reduce forgotten follow-up, strengthen security, and support better decisions, it can give people back some of the attention the modern workday stole.

A healthy AI-era business should not feel like everyone is sprinting forever. It should feel clearer. It should feel more visible. People should know where work lives, who owns the next step, what has been promised, what is waiting, and what needs a human decision. The business may move quickly, but it should not feel like a room full of invisible alarms.

That is one of the reasons I care so much about building from a security-first mindset. When you build a system with security in mind, you learn to respect boundaries. Who should have access? What should be logged? What should require approval? What information should not be exposed? What change should trigger a review? Those are technical questions, yes, but they are also human questions. Boundaries are not just about keeping threats out. They are about keeping the business from becoming a place where everything touches everybody all the time.

The old workday had boundaries by default. The new workday needs boundaries by design.

What ends and what begins

So what exactly is ending? Not work. Not ambition. Not service. Not excellence. Not the need to show up and do hard things. What is ending is the assumption that a business can rely on a loose collection of human habits to manage a machine-speed environment.

The old workday assumed that the day itself would help organize the work. Morning for messages. Midday for meetings. Afternoon for follow-up. End of day for closing the loop. That still happens in some places, and there is nothing wrong with structure. But the modern business stream no longer respects that sequence. Important information can arrive at any time. Routine information can pretend to be important. AI can create output faster than the approval process can handle it. Customers can form opinions before you realize they are waiting. Security issues can happen outside the hours when someone is paying attention.

That means the business has to mature. It has to know what needs immediate response and what needs scheduled review. It has to know which decisions can be delegated and which ones need the owner. It has to know which tasks should be automated and which conversations should remain personal. It has to know when speed is helping and when speed is hiding sloppiness under a shiny surface.

This is not a gloomy message. I actually think it is hopeful. Because once you stop trying to preserve a workday that no longer exists, you can build something better. You can design a rhythm that fits the real world. You can stop apologizing for not being able to hold every detail in your head. You can stop letting every notification vote on your priorities. You can stop mistaking availability for leadership.

Availability says, 'I can be reached.' Leadership says, 'I know what deserves my attention.' Those are not the same thing.

The end of the old workday is an invitation to become more deliberate. It asks you to decide how information enters your business, how decisions move, how customers are cared for, how your team communicates, how AI is allowed to help, and where human judgment remains non-negotiable. That is not less human. That is more human because it stops asking people to survive on scattered attention and starts giving leadership a structure to stand on.

That is where the next chapter takes us. Because once the workday becomes a stream, software stops being something people only use. It starts becoming something that participates in the work itself. And when software becomes a worker, the leader has to understand what kind of authority it has been given.

The old workday ended when work became a constant stream. The new advantage belongs to businesses that protect attention, design rhythm, and keep human judgment in charge of machine-speed systems.

Part One - What Changed

Chapter 3

When Software Became a Worker

There was a time when software was quiet. It sat on the computer until someone opened it. It stored files, sent invoices, organized calendars, processed payroll, held customer records, and reminded us of appointments. It was useful, sometimes frustrating, often expensive, but still mostly passive. Software waited for a person to tell it what to do.

That version of software shaped an entire generation of business. The leader made the decision. The employee entered the information. The system saved the result. If something needed to be reviewed, someone had to go look for it. If something needed to be sent, someone had to press the button. If something needed to be corrected, someone had to notice the mistake first.

Then something changed. Quietly at first, then all at once. Software stopped only storing information and started doing something with it. It began suggesting the next step. It began drafting the message. It began sorting the inbox, flagging the risk, predicting the customer, recommending the response, summarizing the meeting, generating the report, and watching for the pattern. In other words, software started acting less like a filing cabinet and more like a worker.

That is one of the biggest shifts in the AI era, and it is also one of the easiest to underestimate. We are not simply buying better tools. We are inviting a new kind of labor into the business. Not human labor. Not emotional labor. Not judgment in the way people carry judgment. But labor all the same.

For the average business owner, this can feel both exciting and unsettling. Exciting because help is always welcome. Unsettling because most businesses were designed for software that waits, not software that acts. And there is a very big difference between a tool that sits still and a system that starts moving work through the business on its own.

Chapter 1 was about business getting faster than people. Chapter 2 was about the old workday turning into a constant stream. Chapter 3 is about what happens next: the tools inside the business begin to participate in the work itself.

Software used to wait for us

To understand why this matters, it helps to remember the old relationship between people and software. A spreadsheet did not wake up in the morning and decide what numbers mattered. A customer relationship system did not reach out to a client unless someone told it to. An accounting platform did not explain what cash flow meant for next month unless a human went in, reviewed the numbers, and made sense of them.

That old arrangement gave people control, but it also created a lot of drag. Every piece of software was its own room. The calendar was one room. Email was another. Accounting was another. Marketing lived somewhere else. Customer service had its own corner. The business owner, manager, or team had to walk from room to room gathering clues.

That is why so many businesses became tool-rich and clarity-poor. They had software for everything, but they still did not have a clean picture. The problem was not always a lack of technology. Many businesses had plenty of technology. The problem was that the technology was waiting in separate places, and the human had to become the bridge.

AI begins to change that relationship because AI does not only hold information. It can interpret, connect, summarize, compare, and act on information. That does not mean it always does those things correctly. It does not mean it should be trusted without review. But it does mean the role of software has changed. It is no longer just a place where work is stored. It is becoming part of how work gets done.

The quiet promotion nobody announced

One of the strangest things about this shift is that most businesses promoted software without realizing it. Nobody called a staff meeting and said, 'Starting today, this platform is no longer just a tool. It is now part of the team.' But that is effectively what happened.

The email platform that drafts a reply is participating. The scheduling tool that recommends available times is participating. The accounting system that flags unusual spending is participating. The customer service platform that suggests a response is participating. The marketing tool that generates campaign language is participating. Little by little, software crossed the line from storage into action.

That line matters because action creates consequences. A stored document can be wrong and sit there quietly. A sent message can create confusion. A mislabeled customer can change the way the business treats that person. A poor recommendation can lead a leader into the wrong decision. A generated report can sound confident while missing the context that only a human would know.

This is why I do not like the phrase 'just use AI' as business advice. It sounds bold, but it is incomplete. Use AI where? For what? With whose approval? Using what data? Under what rules? With what kind of review? Those questions may not sound glamorous, but they are the questions that separate a disciplined AI-era business from a chaotic one.

AI changed the job description of software

The old job description for software was simple: help people do the work. The new job description is more complicated: help people do the work, notice what people might miss, move routine tasks forward, and sometimes create the first version of a decision for a human to approve.

That last part is where the AI era becomes powerful. It is also where it becomes dangerous. A first draft can save time. A first recommendation can sharpen thinking. A first summary can help a leader see faster. But a first draft is not the same as truth. A first recommendation is not the same as wisdom. A first summary is not the same as understanding.

Imagine a small business owner who receives a long customer complaint. AI can summarize the issue, pull out the main frustration, suggest a response, and even identify whether the tone is angry, disappointed, confused, or urgent.

That is helpful. But AI may not know that this customer has been loyal for seven years. It may not know that the last problem was caused by a supplier, not the staff. It may not know that the customer is embarrassed and needs dignity more than a discount.

That is why the human role does not disappear. It changes. The leader is no longer only the person doing every task by hand. The leader becomes the person who sets the operating standard, decides what the software may handle, reviews what matters, and protects the trust that automation can accidentally damage.

A worker without a role becomes a risk

Every business owner has seen what happens when people are placed in unclear roles. One person thinks someone else handled the client. A manager assumes the invoice was sent. A team member updates a file but nobody knows which version is final. Confusion does not always come from laziness. Sometimes it comes from unclear responsibility.

The same thing happens with software. When an AI tool is added to a business without a clear role, it creates invisible confusion. Is it drafting only, or is it sending? Is it summarizing only, or is it deciding priority? Is it suggesting a customer segment, or is it changing who gets contacted? Is it allowed to use private business data? Is anyone checking what it produces?

A lot of risk hides inside those small questions. Not because AI is evil. Not because technology is the enemy. Because any worker without a role can make a mess, and software can make that mess faster than a person can see it happening.

This is especially important for small businesses because small teams often rely on informal knowledge. The owner knows the exceptions. The office manager knows which client needs extra patience. The sales lead knows which vendor always runs late. Informal knowledge can keep a small business alive, but AI does not automatically inherit it. If that knowledge is not written, structured, protected, and reviewed, the software may operate on an incomplete version of the business.

The invisible org chart now includes systems

Most people think of an org chart as a picture of people. The owner at the top. Managers beneath that. Teams beneath them. Maybe departments, contractors, vendors, or partners. But in the AI era, that picture is incomplete. The invisible org chart now includes systems.

Your billing system has influence. Your customer service software has influence. Your marketing automation has influence. Your AI assistant has influence. Your security tools have influence. Your calendar, inbox, file storage, payment processor, website, and analytics all shape what the business sees, ignores, prioritizes, and responds to.

That does not mean a piece of software is a person. It means the system affects behavior. It changes what gets attention. It changes what feels urgent. It changes what the team believes is true. A dashboard can make a number look more important than it is. A notification can pull a leader away from deeper work. A generated message can sound polished enough to hide that it is not right.

In a healthy AI-era business, systems should support leadership, not replace it. They should make the truth easier to see, not harder. They should reduce repetitive drag, not create a new fog of automated activity. They should help the business move faster while making responsibility clearer.

The difference between help and authority

One of the cleanest ways to think about AI in business is to separate help from authority. Help means the system assists. Authority means the system decides or acts in a way that affects the business, the customer, the money, the reputation, or the risk.

A system that drafts a proposal is helping. A system that sends the proposal to a high-value client without review has authority. A system that summarizes expenses is helping. A system that approves payment has authority. A system that flags a customer issue is helping. A system that closes the complaint without human oversight has authority.

This distinction is not meant to scare people away from AI. It is meant to make AI usable in a serious business. Most business owners do not need fear. They need categories. They need a way to look at a tool and say, 'This can help here, but it should not have authority there.'

Mature companies do not only ask whether a system can do something. They ask whether it should. They ask what happens if it is wrong. They ask who is responsible for the outcome. They ask whether the customer would still trust the business if the process were visible.

Software should make the business more human, not less

Here is the part I want every reader to hear clearly: using AI well does not mean making the business colder. It should do the opposite. Good automation should remove the repetitive weight that keeps people from doing the work only people can do.

When software handles the routine summary, the human can spend more attention on the real conversation. When software organizes the customer history, the owner can respond with more care. When software notices a pattern in late invoices, the leader can address the cash flow before panic sets in. When software prepares the first draft, the human can make it true, kind, sharp, and appropriate.

That is the promise. But the promise only works when the business stays honest about what software is and is not. AI can help with language, speed, pattern recognition, and organization. It can help a leader see sooner. It can reduce the blank-page problem. But it does not carry your values unless you build those values into the way it is used.

A business that cares about customers must teach its systems to protect customers. A business that cares about privacy must design privacy into its workflows. A business that cares about accuracy must create review points. A business that cares about reputation must not let automation speak in its name without standards.

The new leadership skill is supervision at scale

As software becomes more active, leaders need a skill that used to belong mostly to managers of people: supervision.

Not hovering. Not micromanaging every click. Real supervision. The ability to define the work, set the standard, observe the output, correct the drift, and improve the system over time.

In the AI era, supervision at scale means the leader does not personally do every small thing, but also does not disappear from responsibility. The leader decides which tasks can be accelerated. The leader decides which work requires approval. The leader decides what data should never be casually fed into a tool. The leader decides how often the system is reviewed.

This is not glamorous work, but it is powerful work. It is the difference between a business that merely experiments with AI and a business that can actually operate with AI. Experiments are easy. Operating is harder. Operating requires rhythm, rules, ownership, and review.

That is where many leaders will separate themselves. The flashy conversation will always chase the newest app. The serious conversation will ask whether the business is becoming clearer, safer, faster, and more trustworthy because of the system. If the answer is no, the tool is not an advantage yet. It is just activity.

What this means for the business owner

If you are reading this as a business owner, I do not want you to feel like you are late. I want you to feel like you are looking at the right thing. You do not need to master every AI tool on the market. You do not need to speak like a machine learning engineer. You do not need to pretend you are excited about every new feature that appears in your inbox.

What you do need is a new mental model. Software is no longer only something your people use. In many cases, it is something that participates in the work your people do. That means it deserves placement. It deserves rules. It deserves review. It deserves a clear relationship to human judgment.

Start with the places where software is already acting in your business. Where is it drafting? Where is it sorting? Where is it recommending? Where is it routing? Where is it flagging? Where is it making the first version of something a person used to create from scratch? Those are the places where the invisible org chart has already changed.

Then ask a better question than 'Are we using AI?' Ask, 'Are we supervising the systems that now shape our work?' That question will take you much further. It will help you protect trust. It will help you reduce confusion. It will help you build a business that moves faster without becoming careless.

Software used to wait for people. Now it participates in the work. The advantage belongs to businesses that treat active software like a supervised worker: useful, powerful, bounded, reviewed, and never confused with human judgment.

Part One - What Changed

Chapter 4

The New Divide: Operators vs. Survivors

For a long time, people talked about business competition as if it came down to size. Big companies had more money, more staff, more systems, and more room to make mistakes. Small companies had to be scrappy. Local companies had to be personal. Startups had to be fast. Family businesses had to be trusted. Everyone knew their lane, even if the lane was hard.

The AI era changes that picture. It does not erase the advantages of money, staff, and scale. Those things still matter. But it introduces a new divide that cuts across every size of business, every industry, and every level of experience. The divide is not simply between companies that use AI and companies that do not. Plenty of businesses are using AI badly. Plenty of businesses have bought tools without becoming stronger.

The real divide is between operators and survivors.

Operators build businesses that can see, decide, act, measure, protect, and improve. Survivors spend their days reacting to whatever is loudest. Operators create rhythm. Survivors chase urgency. Operators make the business easier to understand over time. Survivors keep carrying the whole thing in their head and hope nothing falls out.

I do not use the word survivor as an insult. Many honest, hardworking business owners are surviving because the old way of operating stopped being enough before anyone gave them a better one. They are talented people running companies in a world where the speed of the work changed, the number of tools exploded, and the pressure never really turns off.

But the fact that survival is understandable does not make it sustainable. Chapter 4 is where we name the choice every business now faces: will the company become an operator, or will it keep surviving by force of will until the market exposes the weakness?

The divide is not technical

One of the biggest mistakes in the AI conversation is assuming that the winners will be the most technical people. Technical ability helps, of course. A business that understands systems, data, automation, and cybersecurity has an advantage. But technical knowledge by itself does not create a strong company. A person can understand software and still run a chaotic business.

The more important question is whether the business can operate. Can it turn information into action without losing its mind? Can it serve customers consistently? Can it protect sensitive information? Can it tell the difference between what is urgent and what is important? Can it repeat good work without depending on one exhausted person to remember every detail?

AI does not magically create discipline. It can write faster, summarize faster, sort faster, and recommend faster. But if the business underneath it is unclear, AI simply accelerates the lack of clarity. That is why the new divide is not technical people on one side and nontechnical people on the other. It is disciplined operators on one side and reactive survivors on the other.

Survivors live in reaction

A survival-mode business often looks busier than a healthy one. The phone is ringing. The inbox is full. People are moving. Problems are being solved. The owner is everywhere. Customers still get served. Money still comes in. From the outside, it can look like momentum.

But inside the business, the day feels like a series of fires. The team waits for the owner to answer the same questions again and again. Information lives in text threads, email chains, notebooks, dashboards, and someone's memory. Decisions get made based on whoever noticed the problem first. Work moves forward because people push hard, not because the system is designed well.

Survival mode feels like being needed all the time but never fully in control. It feels like solving the same issue every week in a slightly different outfit. It feels like buying new tools and somehow having more places to check instead of fewer things to worry about. AI can make that feeling worse if the business does not pause long enough to organize itself.

Operators build rhythm

An operator thinks differently. An operator does not ask only, 'How do I get through today?' An operator asks, 'How should this business work so tomorrow is not a repeat of the same chaos?' That question changes everything.

Operators build rhythm into the business. They know when money is reviewed. They know how customer issues move. They know where important documents live. They know who approves what. They know what gets automated, what gets escalated, and what gets recorded. They do not build rhythm because they are boring. They build rhythm because rhythm creates freedom.

A business without rhythm depends on constant personal heroics. Someone has to remember. Someone has to chase. Someone has to rescue the situation. Heroics may feel impressive in the moment, but they are expensive. They drain the owner, confuse the team, and teach the business to rely on emergency energy instead of repeatable strength.

Tool buyers and system builders

A survivor usually becomes a tool buyer first. Something hurts, so the owner looks for a tool to relieve the pain. The inbox is overwhelming, so they buy an email tool. The calendar is messy, so they buy a scheduling tool. Marketing feels behind, so they buy a content tool. Each purchase makes sense in isolation, but isolation is part of the problem.

An operator becomes a system builder. That does not mean the owner builds software from scratch. It means the owner asks how each tool fits into the way the business actually works. Where does the information come from? Who reviews it? What happens next? What should be logged? What should be protected? What should never be automated without approval?

This shift is small in language and enormous in practice. A tool buyer collects features. A system builder creates flow. A tool buyer hopes the product will fix the business. A system builder uses the product to strengthen a process that already has a purpose.

AI rewards the business underneath it

This may be one of the most uncomfortable truths of the AI era: AI rewards the business underneath it. If the business has clean information, clear standards, and responsible leadership, AI can amplify those strengths. If the business has messy data, unclear authority, and weak accountability, AI can amplify those weaknesses too.

Think of AI like a powerful assistant walking into your company on the first day. If the company has documented processes, clear priorities, and a leader who knows what good work looks like, that assistant can become useful quickly. If the company has no clear instructions, scattered information, and five different versions of the truth, the assistant may move fast, but it will move through confusion.

That is why two businesses can use similar tools and get completely different results. One owner uses AI to prepare for meetings, summarize customer history, identify slow processes, improve communication, and make better decisions. Another owner uses AI to generate more content, more emails, more tasks, and more activity without fixing the operating system. The tool may be similar. The business underneath it is not.

Speed exposes discipline

Speed is attractive. Every business wants faster answers, faster service, faster reporting, faster marketing, faster follow-up, and faster decisions. Speed can help a company serve better and compete harder. But speed does not forgive disorder. It reveals it.

When a slow process is messy, the mess is easier to hide. People have time to patch it. Someone can send a clarifying message. Someone can catch the missing detail before the customer sees it. The business may be inefficient, but the inefficiency acts like padding.

AI removes some of that padding. The email goes out faster. The summary circulates faster. The recommendation reaches the leader faster. That can be wonderful when the system is sound. It can be dangerous when the system is careless. Operators understand that faster is only valuable when the business knows where it is going.

The small business advantage

There is good news here, especially for small businesses. The AI era does not have to belong only to giant companies. Large companies have budgets, but they also have bureaucracy. They have departments, legacy systems, politics, approval chains, and habits that can slow down real change. A smaller business can sometimes become an operator faster because it has fewer layers to untangle.

A small business owner can look across the whole company and see the real problems. The owner can notice that customer follow-up is inconsistent, that receipts are disorganized, that scheduling depends too much on one person, that no one knows which tool is the source of truth, or that sensitive information is being handled casually. These are not glamorous discoveries, but they are powerful ones.

When a small business fixes those basics, AI becomes more useful immediately. It can help organize thinking, draft customer communication, summarize financial patterns, support training, prepare content, improve service, and reduce repetitive work. But the owner has to aim it at a real operating problem, not just a vague desire to be current.

The owner cannot be the whole operating system

Many businesses survive because the owner is extraordinary. She remembers the details. He knows the customers. She understands the backstory. He catches the mistake before it becomes public. That kind of leadership is valuable. It is also dangerous when the entire company depends on it.

If the owner is the operating system, the business has a ceiling. Growth becomes harder because every decision has to pass through one mind. Hiring becomes harder because new people cannot access what has never been written down. Automation becomes risky because the tool cannot protect context it was never given. Even rest becomes complicated because the business does not know how to think without the owner present.

This is one of the reasons I care so deeply about business operating systems and security-first structure. In my own work building technology, the question is never just whether a feature can be built. The question is whether the system can be trusted, governed, reviewed, and understood. The same principle applies to any business, even one that never writes a line of code.

From heroic effort to repeatable capability

The move from survivor to operator is the move from heroic effort to repeatable capability. Heroic effort says, 'We got it done because we worked hard.' Repeatable capability says, 'We can get it done well again because the business knows how.'

There is a big difference between those two statements. Hard work matters. Most business owners have carried seasons that required grit, sacrifice, and stubborn faith. But hard work should not be the only thing holding the company together. At some point, the business has to become capable without constant emergency energy.

Repeatable capability is what allows AI to help instead of confuse. When the business has a standard response process, AI can draft within that standard. When the business has a clear approval rule, automation can route work responsibly. When the business has an audit trail, the owner can review what happened instead of guessing.

Trust is where the divide becomes visible

The market may not see your internal systems at first. Customers may not know how your team routes work, stores information, reviews AI output, or protects private details. But they will eventually feel the result.

They will feel it when the business answers clearly. They will feel it when promises are kept. They will feel it when the invoice matches the agreement. They will feel it when their information is handled with care. They will also feel it when the opposite happens.

That is why trust is the place where operators and survivors eventually separate. A survivor may get by for a while on charm, effort, or urgency. An operator builds trust into the way the business works. In the AI era, trust is not soft. Trust is infrastructure.

Becoming an operator is a decision

The good news is that becoming an operator is not a personality type. It is not reserved for the naturally organized, the highly technical, or the people with large staffs. It is a decision followed by a series of disciplined improvements.

It begins when the owner stops asking, 'How do I survive this week?' as the only question and starts asking, 'What would make this business easier to run, easier to trust, and easier to improve?' That question does not solve everything overnight, but it points the business in the right direction.

From there, the path is practical. Pick the areas where confusion repeats. Look at the places where the owner is still the only bridge. Notice the tools that do not talk to each other. Identify the work that should be documented before it is automated. Decide which actions need human approval. Define what good looks like before asking AI to produce more of it.

The AI era is creating a new divide. Not between big businesses and small businesses. Not between technical people and ordinary people. Between operators and survivors. Survivors react until exhaustion becomes the system. Operators build businesses that can see, decide, act, protect, and improve. The businesses that win will not be the ones with the most tools. They will be the ones with the clearest operating discipline behind the tools.

Part One - What Changed

Chapter 5

Trust Is the New Business Currency

For a long time, business owners were taught to think of currency in one way. Money came in. Money went out. Revenue, expenses, payroll, taxes, cash flow, and profit were the numbers that told the story of the company.

Those numbers still matter. I would never tell a business owner to ignore the books. Money is oxygen for a company. But in the AI era, another kind of currency moves through every business, and many people do not notice it until they are already losing it.

That currency is trust.

Trust is what makes a customer click pay now instead of close tab. It is what makes an employee follow a new process instead of quietly working around it. It is what makes a vendor extend grace, a partner sign the agreement, and a leader feel safe using technology instead of feeling like every new tool is a gamble.

AI did not make trust important. Trust was always important. AI simply made trust easier to measure, easier to break, easier to fake, and harder to rebuild once people sense something is wrong.

That is why this chapter belongs at the end of Part One. We have talked about business getting faster than people, the old workday disappearing, software becoming a worker, and the divide between operators and survivors. Under all of those changes is one hidden question: can people still trust what is happening inside and around the business?

Trust used to have more time

In the older version of business, trust often had time to develop. A customer could walk into a store, meet the owner, look around, ask questions, and decide whether the place felt right. A referral might come from a neighbor. A handshake might carry weight. A local reputation could protect a company for years.

That world has not disappeared, but it is no longer the only world businesses live in. Today, a customer may meet your business for the first time through a search result, an automated reply, an online review, a payment link, a short video, or a chatbot. They may decide within seconds whether you look organized, safe, responsive, and real.

That means a business can lose trust before a human being ever has the chance to speak.

The form loads slowly. The invoice looks suspicious. The reply sounds robotic in a way that feels careless. The website says one thing, the email says another, and the customer wonders who is actually in charge. None of those moments may feel dramatic to the business owner, but to the customer they are clues.

People are always reading the room, even online. They are asking, sometimes without realizing it, whether this business can be trusted with their money, their information, their time, their problem, their reputation, or their family.

The customer can feel the system

One of the biggest mistakes leaders make is believing customers only experience the front of the business. They think the customer sees the logo, the product, the sales message, the website, the packaging, or the person at the counter.

Customers experience much more than that. Customers feel the system behind the business.

They feel it when they have to repeat the same information three times. They feel it when nobody can find their order. They feel it when the left hand does not know what the right hand promised. They feel it when an automated message says, 'We care about your experience,' but nobody actually responds for four days.

They also feel it when everything is smooth. They feel it when a business remembers what matters. They feel it when the next step is clear. They feel it when a mistake is handled with honesty instead of excuses. They feel it when the technology supports the relationship instead of replacing the relationship.

That is why AI cannot be treated only as a back-office decision. The tools you choose, the automations you build, the data you collect, the messages you send, and the controls you put in place eventually show up in the customer experience.

A messy system creates a messy feeling. A disciplined system creates confidence.

The customer may not know your software stack, and they may not care which tool sends the email or routes the ticket. But they can feel whether the business is paying attention. They can feel whether the company is making their life easier or asking them to carry the weight of the company's confusion.

Speed without proof becomes noise

AI gives businesses the ability to move faster. Faster writing. Faster summaries. Faster proposals. Faster marketing. Faster customer service. Faster internal communication. That speed can be useful when it is pointed in the right direction.

There is nothing noble about wasting three hours on a task that can be handled safely in fifteen minutes. There is nothing impressive about making customers wait because the business refuses to improve.

But speed by itself is not the advantage people think it is.

In a machine-speed world, everyone can sound quick. Everyone can produce more content. Everyone can answer more messages. Everyone can generate a polished paragraph, a clean image, a sharper pitch, or a professional-looking proposal. The question is not only who can move fast. The question is who can be trusted while moving fast.

That is where proof enters the picture. Proof is the receipt, the record, the audit trail, the clear policy, the consistent answer, the documented approval, the secure process. Proof is the part of trust that does not depend on personality.

A business that moves quickly but cannot prove what happened becomes noisy. The customer was promised something, but nobody knows who approved it. The AI tool created an answer, but nobody checked whether it was true.

A complaint was handled, but the pattern was never reviewed.

That kind of speed eventually becomes expensive. It creates rework, refunds, disputes, confusion, burnout, and risk. More importantly, it teaches customers and employees not to rely on the system. Trust grows when speed and proof travel together.

Inside the business, trust becomes oxygen

When people talk about business trust, they usually talk about customers. That makes sense, because customers keep the lights on. But some of the most important trust in a company happens behind the scenes.

A team needs to trust the information it is given. A manager needs to trust that a report means what it says. A bookkeeper needs to trust that expenses are categorized correctly. A salesperson needs to trust that the lead information is current. A founder needs to trust that the dashboard is not hiding a disaster under pretty colors.

Without that internal trust, every decision gets slower. People double-check what should already be clear. They ask the same questions again and again. They build side spreadsheets because they do not trust the main system. They keep private notes because the official process does not feel reliable.

This is one of the quiet costs of a disorganized business. It does not only waste time. It trains people to doubt the business itself.

AI can either improve that situation or make it worse. If AI is connected to clean information, clear rules, and human judgment, it can help the business move with more confidence. It can summarize what matters, surface patterns, route decisions, and reduce the mental load on people.

If AI is connected to confusion, it can produce confident confusion at scale. It can make the wrong answer sound polished. It can repeat outdated information with authority. It can create the feeling that something has been handled when, in reality, no one owns the outcome.

That is why trust is not only a brand issue. It is an operations issue.

AI raises the trust standard

A lot of leaders are still asking whether AI is trustworthy. That is a fair question, but it is not the only question. The deeper question is whether the business using AI is trustworthy.

The same tool can be helpful in one company and dangerous in another. In one business, AI may draft a response that a trained person reviews before sending. In another, AI may be allowed to answer customers about refunds, health, finance, legal language, security, or personal information without the right guardrails.

The difference is not the tool alone. The difference is the standard around the tool.

This is where leadership returns to the center of the conversation. AI does not remove responsibility from the owner, founder, executive, or manager. It makes responsibility more visible. If the system gives bad information, who checked it? If customer data is placed into the wrong tool, who allowed it? If an automation sends the wrong message, who approved the process?

Those questions should not make a business owner freeze. They should make the owner build better structure.

The trust standard in the AI era is not perfection. Perfection is not realistic. The standard is responsibility. Can the business explain what it is doing? Can it show who has access? Can it protect sensitive information? Can it correct mistakes quickly? Can it prove that humans are still accountable for the decisions that matter?

That is what separates a business using AI wisely from a business playing with fire and calling it innovation.

Confidence lowers friction

In practical terms, trust turns into confidence. Confidence is what people feel when the business behaves consistently enough that they do not have to brace themselves.

A customer has confidence when they believe the payment page is safe, the delivery promise is real, the support process works, and the company will not disappear after the sale. An employee has confidence when priorities are clear, tools are reliable, and the leader does not change direction every time a new app trends online.

Confidence lowers friction. It makes decisions easier. It makes people more willing to buy, refer, renew, collaborate, and forgive occasional mistakes.

This matters because the AI era is full of friction dressed up as convenience. People are asked to create accounts, accept policies, upload documents, trust automated replies, click links, share data, and believe that a company they may never meet in person will handle the details correctly.

Every one of those moments is a small trust transaction. The customer is paying with attention before they pay with money. The employee is paying with effort before they pay with loyalty. The market is paying with belief before it pays with growth.

When a business honors those trust transactions, it builds confidence. When it automates them carelessly, it spends trust faster than it earns it.

Trust is designed, not decorated

Some companies try to solve trust with messaging. They put words like secure, reliable, transparent, customer-first, or AI-powered on the website and hope the language does the work.

Words matter. A business should know how to explain what it stands for. But trust cannot survive as a slogan if the experience contradicts it.

If a company says it values privacy but asks customers for unnecessary information, trust weakens. If it says it is responsive but leaves people waiting without updates, trust weakens. If it says AI makes the business smarter but uses AI to avoid responsibility, trust weakens.

The customer may not use those exact words. They may simply say, 'Something feels off.' In business, that sentence is expensive.

The strongest companies in the AI era will understand that trust is not what the business claims. Trust is what the business proves repeatedly, especially when nobody is clapping, especially when the mistake would be easy to hide, especially when speed is tempting the team to skip the review.

Visible trust usually comes from invisible discipline. Customers cannot see whether passwords are managed responsibly, whether employee access is removed when someone leaves, whether sensitive data is copied into random tools, or whether AI-generated content is reviewed before it goes out. But sooner or later, they feel the consequences.

A disciplined business does not wait for a public problem to decide trust matters. It builds trust into the operating rhythm. It decides what should be automated and what should never be automated without approval. It decides who can access what, how decisions are logged, and how the business will know whether the system is helping or hurting.

The technology is new. The principle is old. Responsible people build responsible systems.

The businesses people will believe

As AI becomes more common, the novelty will fade. At first, people are impressed when a company uses AI at all. Then they become overwhelmed because everyone is using it. Eventually, AI will be expected, just like email, websites, digital payments, and online scheduling became expected.

When that happens, the advantage will not belong to the company that simply says, 'We use AI.' The advantage will belong to the company that uses AI in a way people can trust.

People will choose businesses that make life easier without making them feel exposed. They will choose companies that move quickly without becoming careless. They will choose leaders who use technology without surrendering judgment. They will choose systems that feel clear, safe, and human, even when machines are helping behind the scenes.

This is the heart of building business in the AI era. It is not about becoming less human. It is about building systems strong enough that your humanity can actually show up. When the business is drowning in confusion, the owner has less energy for creativity, care, leadership, and vision. When the business has structure, the human part gets room to breathe.

Trust is the currency that makes that possible.

So before we move into the next part of this book and talk about how the system works now, I want to leave you with this thought: AI may change the speed of business, but trust will decide whether that speed turns into growth or damage.

The future will not only reward businesses that can do more. It will reward businesses that can be believed.

Part Two - How the System Works Now

Part Two - How the System Works Now

Chapter 6

AI Is Not a Tool. It Is an Operating Layer.

Most people meet AI the same way they meet any new piece of software. They hear about a tool. They create an account. They type something into a box. They get an answer back. If the answer is impressive, they think, okay, this is useful. If the answer is strange, they think, maybe this is not ready yet.

That is a normal way to begin. It is also too small a way to think about what is happening.

If AI were only another tool, we could treat it like another app on the desktop. We could use it sometimes, ignore it when we were busy, and decide later whether it belongs in the company. But the shift taking place is much bigger than that. AI is not simply sitting beside the business. It is beginning to sit underneath the way the business works.

That difference matters. A tool helps you do a task. An operating layer changes how tasks connect, how information moves, how decisions are shaped, and how quickly the business can respond. A hammer is a tool. Electricity is a layer. You can put down the hammer. Electricity changes what the whole building can do.

AI is moving in that direction. It is being added into email, calendars, search, customer service, bookkeeping, design, sales, hiring, training, cybersecurity, analytics, document review, and project management. It is not staying in one neat little box where the owner can say, 'We use AI over there.' It is spreading across the business the way electricity spread through buildings, the way the internet spread through offices, and the way smartphones spread through the workday.

That does not mean every business should panic. It means every business needs better language. Once you understand AI as an operating layer, the conversation changes. You stop asking only, 'Which tool should I buy?' and you start asking, 'What part of the business will this touch, what decisions will it influence, what information will it use, and who is still responsible?'

The app is not the point

The easiest mistake in the AI era is to chase the app and miss the architecture. A new platform gets attention. A new feature shows up. A competitor posts about a workflow. A friend says a certain tool changed everything. Suddenly the owner feels pressure to sign up for one more thing.

That is how businesses end up with technology clutter instead of technology strategy.

The app may be useful, but the app is not the point. The point is what the app changes inside the business. Does it shorten a handoff? Does it improve a decision? Does it reduce repetitive work? Does it make information easier to find? Does it protect sensitive data? Does it help the customer feel served, or does it only help the company feel busy?

A business owner can buy ten AI tools and still not have an AI-ready business. The tools may not talk to each other. The data may be messy. The team may not know when to use them. Nobody may be checking the output. The customer may experience none of the promised improvement.

When AI is understood as an operating layer, the leader stops collecting shiny objects and starts designing flow. The goal is not to have the most tools. The goal is to have a business that can see clearly, decide wisely, act faster, protect trust, and learn from what happens.

A layer sits between work and outcome

Think about the parts of a normal business day. A message comes in. Someone reads it. They decide whether it matters. They look for context. They write a response. They update a record. They schedule a follow-up. They tell another person. They save a document. They make a decision. They hope nothing was missed.

For years, software helped with pieces of that process. Email held the message. A CRM held the customer record. A calendar held the appointment. A spreadsheet held the numbers. A project tool held the tasks. The human being was the bridge between all of it.

That bridge was exhausting.

People had to remember where things lived. They had to copy information from one place to another. They had to reread old threads, search folders, interpret dashboards, and keep mental notes about what was really going on. The business often depended on one person remembering the invisible connections between systems.

AI changes that because it can sit in the middle of those connections. It can summarize, sort, draft, compare, flag, recommend, classify, translate, search, and surface patterns.

Instead of waiting for a person to manually pull meaning out of ten places, AI can help bring meaning closer to the moment of action.

That is powerful. It is also dangerous if the business does not know what the layer is doing.

A layer shapes what people see. It can decide which customer request looks urgent, which resume looks relevant, which invoice looks unusual, which security alert looks serious, or which paragraph sounds polished enough to send. If the layer is working well, it reduces noise and helps people focus. If the layer is poorly governed, it can hide important signals behind confident suggestions.

This is the reason leaders cannot treat AI like a toy sitting on the side of the desk. Once AI starts influencing the path from work to outcome, it becomes part of the operating system of the business.

The owner still owns the standard

One of the most comforting myths about technology is that the tool will carry the standard for us. If the software is advanced enough, maybe it will make the process mature. If the automation is clever enough, maybe it will make the team disciplined. If the AI sounds professional enough, maybe it will make the business credible.

It will not.

AI can strengthen a standard that already exists. It can help enforce a process that has been clearly designed. It can make good judgment easier to apply at scale. But it cannot invent the moral, operational, or customer-service standard of the business.

If a company does not know how it wants customers treated, AI will not know either. If a company has never defined what information is sensitive, AI cannot magically protect it. If a leader has not decided what requires human approval, the system may move too much too quickly. If a team has no shared definition of quality, AI can produce output that looks polished while missing the point.

The owner still owns the standard.

A mature business asks different questions before it hands work to AI. What does good look like here? What must never be guessed? What needs a human review? What data should not be entered into this system? What should be logged? What should be escalated? What would damage trust if this went wrong?

Those questions are not anti-technology. They are how serious businesses use technology without losing control of themselves.

AI makes the business brain visible

Every business has a brain, even if nobody has named it. The business brain is not one person. It is the way information, rules, habits, memory, and judgment come together to produce decisions.

In a small business, that brain may live mostly in the owner. The owner knows which customer always pays late, which vendor needs a reminder, which employee is overwhelmed, which expense is unusual, and which promise should never be made without checking the calendar. The problem is that when the brain lives only in the owner, the business cannot scale without wearing that person down.

AI exposes that arrangement. It shows where the business has clean knowledge and where it only has memory, habit, and hope.

When a company tries to use AI and the results are weak, the tool is not always the problem. Sometimes the tool is revealing that the business has never organized its own knowledge. The policies are unclear. The data is incomplete. The process lives in somebody's head. The customer information is spread across systems. The approvals are informal. The exceptions are handled differently every time.

In that sense, AI can become a mirror. It reflects the quality of the business brain.

A disciplined business can use AI to make that brain more visible and useful. It can create better summaries, better handoffs, better alerts, better training, better records, and better decision support. A disorganized business may use AI and discover that the machine is simply amplifying the disorganization. That is not failure. That is a diagnosis.

The leader who understands this does not get embarrassed by the diagnosis. She gets to work.

The invisible handoffs matter most

Most breakdowns in business do not happen because one dramatic thing goes wrong. They happen in the handoffs. The customer asked a question, but sales assumed support would answer. Support assumed operations already knew. Operations assumed the invoice had been updated. Finance assumed the contract was final. Leadership assumed the dashboard was current.

Every assumption is a tiny crack. At slow speed, people may have enough time to catch the crack before it becomes visible. At machine speed, the crack travels faster.

This is where AI as an operating layer can help if it is designed properly. It can watch for patterns, remind the right person, draft the next step, flag missing information, and keep context attached to the work. It can reduce the number of times a human being has to carry the whole process in memory.

But again, the layer must be governed. If AI is added to a broken handoff without redesigning the responsibility around it, the business may only automate the confusion. A reminder goes to the wrong person faster. A response is drafted before the facts are checked. A task closes because the system thinks it is complete, but the customer still does not have what they need.

That is why AI readiness is not only a technology project. It is an operations project. It asks the business to look at the places where work moves from person to person, system to system, promise to delivery, and ask whether the path is clear enough for machines to assist without making a mess.

The invisible handoffs are where trust is either protected or lost.

From scattered tools to a control layer

A business with scattered tools can still function. Many do. The owner knows the password. The manager knows the workaround. The bookkeeper knows which spreadsheet is real. The customer service person knows which inbox matters most. The company keeps moving because people compensate for the weakness of the system.

But compensation is not the same as control.

A control layer gives the business a clearer way to see what matters. It does not mean everything has to be expensive, complicated, or enterprise-grade on day one. It means the business knows where decisions live, where sensitive information goes, who can access what, how work is tracked, and how leaders know whether the system is healthy.

AI belongs inside that control layer, not floating randomly around it. When AI is scattered, it becomes another source of uncertainty. When AI is integrated with rules, visibility, and accountability, it becomes a force multiplier.

That kind of business feels different from the inside. The owner is not guessing as much. The team is not hunting as much. The customer is not repeating themselves as much. The leader can see patterns sooner. Problems are not hidden until they become emergencies.

That is the promise of AI when it is treated seriously: not magic, not replacement, not chaos, but a stronger layer of awareness and action underneath the business.

Do not confuse assistance with authority

There is a line every AI-ready business has to understand. AI can assist. It should not automatically become the authority.

That line matters because AI often sounds confident. It can produce a clean paragraph even when the information underneath is incomplete. It can summarize a problem without understanding the emotional weight behind it. It can suggest a decision without carrying the responsibility for the outcome.

A human being has to know when confidence is not the same as truth.

This does not make AI useless. It makes AI powerful in the correct role. A good assistant can save time, organize thoughts, surface options, and reduce friction. A reckless authority can create liability, damage relationships, and teach people to stop thinking.

The businesses that handle AI well will decide ahead of time where the machine can move freely and where it must pause for a person. They will not make that decision because they are afraid of the future. They will make it because they respect the weight of trust.

The new operating question

In the old software era, the question was often, 'What tool do we need?' That question still has a place. Businesses need tools. They need email platforms, payment systems, accounting software, calendars, security controls, customer records, and communication channels.

But the AI era adds a better question: 'How should the business think, move, and protect itself now that machines can participate in the work?'

That question is larger, and that is why it is more useful. It does not let the owner hide behind a purchase. It brings the conversation back to design. It asks how information enters the business, how it is verified, how decisions are made, how work is assigned, how customers are served, how mistakes are caught, and how trust is preserved.

This is the mindset shift at the center of Part Two. We are not talking about AI as a clever shortcut. We are talking about AI as part of the modern business operating environment. Once you see it that way, you become more careful, but you also become more capable. You can stop reacting to every new tool and start building a business that knows how to absorb new technology without losing its shape.

That is what leadership looks like in the AI era. Not knowing every technical detail. Not chasing every trend. Not pretending machines are magic. Leadership is deciding what the business stands for, how it works, what it protects, and where technology belongs inside that structure.

AI is not a tool you occasionally use when you have extra time. It is becoming a layer in the environment where business now happens. The sooner a leader understands that, the sooner the business can stop being surprised by the future and start operating with intention.

The next chapter takes that idea one step further. If AI is becoming an operating layer, then every modern business needs a control room. Not a room full of screens for show, but a way to see the truth early enough to act on it.

Part Two - How the System Works Now

Chapter 7
The Modern Business Control Room

Every serious business needs a place where the truth comes together.

I do not mean a dramatic room with giant screens on the wall, people wearing headsets, and someone yelling, 'Zoom in on sector seven.' That looks impressive in movies, but most businesses do not need a Hollywood command center. They need something much more practical and much more powerful. They need a way to see what is happening before the damage is obvious.

That is the modern business control room.

It may live inside a dashboard, a secure platform, a weekly leadership rhythm, a set of alerts, or a combination of systems that all point back to one source of operational truth. The form can change. The purpose does not. A control room helps a business see its money, customers, people, operations, risks, promises, and decisions in time to act.

Without that, leaders are not really leading the business. They are chasing it. And in the AI era, chasing the business is not enough. The pace is too fast, the information is too scattered, and the risks travel too quietly.

This is why a control room is not a luxury idea for big companies. It is a survival idea for modern companies.

You cannot manage what you cannot see

Business owners are often told they need to work on the business, not just in the business. That advice is true, but it is incomplete. You cannot work on a business you cannot see clearly.

If the numbers are late, the owner is guessing. If customer issues are buried in inboxes, the owner is guessing. If employee workload lives in hallway conversations, the owner is guessing. If security concerns are handled only when something breaks, the owner is guessing. If tasks are spread across five platforms and nobody knows which one is the real source of truth, the whole company is guessing together.

Guessing can feel normal when a business is young. In the early days, the owner often survives on instinct. She knows the customers by name. She knows who owes money. She knows which vendor is slow. She knows which employee is struggling. She knows which promises are risky because she made most of them herself.

That works for a while because the business is small enough to fit inside one person's head. Then the business grows, the tools multiply, the customers increase, the team expands, and suddenly the owner's brain becomes the bottleneck. Not because she is weak, but because no human being was designed to be the filing cabinet, fire alarm, traffic controller, customer historian, financial analyst, security monitor, and emotional support system for an entire company.

A control room gives the business a place to breathe. It takes what used to be invisible and starts making it visible. It turns scattered activity into patterns. It turns isolated problems into signals. It turns vague pressure into something the leader can name. That is where better decisions begin.

A dashboard is not always a control room

A lot of businesses already have dashboards. They have sales dashboards, accounting dashboards, project dashboards, marketing dashboards, payroll dashboards, and security dashboards. The problem is that a dashboard by itself is not a control room.

A dashboard shows information. A control room helps the business understand what that information means and what should happen next.

A modern business control room is different. It does not exist to impress people. It exists to reduce surprise.

The control room starts with questions

Before a business can build a useful control room, it has to ask better questions. Technology can collect information, but leadership has to decide what information deserves attention.

The first question is simple: what do we need to know early?

That word early is important. A business does not need a control room so it can admire the wreckage after the fact. It needs a control room so it can see small changes before they turn into expensive problems.

A late invoice is not only a finance issue if it affects payroll. A frustrated customer is not only a support issue if the same complaint appears five times. A missed task is not only an operations issue if it reveals that nobody owns the handoff. A strange login is not only an IT issue if it points to a security risk.

Good leaders learn to see across categories. That is one of the reasons AI matters so much. AI can help connect signals that used to sit in separate rooms. It can summarize what changed, surface patterns, compare behavior, and draw attention to what a busy human might overlook.

But the machine still needs leadership. If the business has not defined what matters, AI may surface what is loud instead of what is important. It may highlight activity instead of progress. It may summarize noise and make it sound like insight. The control room begins when the leader decides what the business must never miss.

The four windows every business needs

Even though every business is different, most modern companies need visibility through four basic windows: customers, money, operations, and risk. Together, those windows tell a leader whether the business is healthy, trusted, and capable of keeping its promises.

The customer window shows what people are actually experiencing. Are questions being answered? Are complaints repeating? Are expectations clear? Are customers being handed from person to person without context? Are promises being made faster than the company can fulfill them?

The money window shows whether the business is financially awake. It is not enough to know that sales came in. The leader needs to understand cash timing, unpaid invoices, recurring expenses, margin pressure, refund patterns, subscriptions that quietly grew, and the difference between revenue that looks good and profit that actually supports the business.

The operations window shows how work moves. It reveals bottlenecks, dropped handoffs, unclear ownership, delayed approvals, overloaded people, and places where the same problem keeps getting solved manually because nobody has fixed the process underneath it.

The risk window shows what can hurt trust. That includes cybersecurity, access control, sensitive data, compliance obligations, vendor exposure, contract mistakes, public reputation, and anything that could damage the business if it went unseen for too long.

A small business may not need a complicated system for all of this on day one. But it does need the discipline of looking. The habit matters before the software becomes sophisticated.

AI makes the control room smarter

This is where AI becomes practical instead of abstract. AI can help a business control room become more than a collection of reports.

Used well, AI gives leaders a better listening system.

But listening is not the same as obeying. The business should not blindly accept every AI conclusion. It should use AI to bring issues closer to the surface, then apply human judgment where the stakes require it. The goal is not to remove people from leadership. The goal is to stop wasting human leadership on preventable confusion.

That kind of clarity changes the emotional temperature of a business. Less panic. Less blame. Less hunting. More ownership.

Control is not the same as control freak

Some people hear the word control and immediately feel resistance. They picture micromanagement. They picture a leader watching every move, questioning every decision, and turning the workplace into a pressure cooker.

That is not the kind of control I am talking about.

Healthy control is not about squeezing people. It is about protecting the business from unnecessary blindness. It is about making sure the right people can see the right information at the right time. It is about reducing chaos so good people can do good work without carrying the entire company in their memory.

A control room should not make the team feel watched in a creepy way. It should make the team feel supported by clarity. People should know what matters, where the work stands, who owns the next step, and how issues get escalated before they become personal emergencies.

The modern control room removes friction by making reality easier to see.

The owner needs one clean version of the truth

One of the most dangerous phrases in business is 'Which version is correct?'

Which spreadsheet is correct? Which number is correct? Which customer note is correct? Which task list is correct? Which contract is final? Which report did the team use?

Which email has the latest decision? Every time a business asks that question, it loses time and trust.

A control room does not mean every piece of information lives in one software product. That may not be realistic. But it does mean the business has rules for truth. It knows where final decisions are recorded. It knows where customer commitments live. It knows which system owns financial truth. It knows how access is controlled. It knows what gets logged. It knows how the team can tell the difference between a draft, a discussion, and a decision.

This is especially important when AI enters the picture. If AI is pulling from messy sources, it can confidently produce messy conclusions. If it is summarizing outdated notes, it can make old information sound current. If it is drafting from incomplete context, it can create polished confusion.

Clean truth makes AI more useful. Messy truth makes AI more risky. That is why business leaders cannot separate AI strategy from data discipline.

Aetis and the control layer mindset

This is also part of the reason I think about business technology differently. I do not see the future as a pile of disconnected apps with AI sprinkled on top. I see the future as a control layer.

That is the mindset behind the kind of work I have been building with Aetis. The point is not to make business feel more complicated. The point is to make the hidden parts of business easier to see, protect, and operate. Security, workflow, money, records, people, and decisions should not live as separate worlds that only meet when something goes wrong. They should support one another.

A business that cannot see risk cannot protect itself. A business that cannot see money clearly cannot grow responsibly. A business that cannot see work clearly cannot serve customers consistently. A business that cannot see decisions clearly cannot hold itself accountable.

This does not mean every reader needs to build a technology platform. Most will not. But every reader can adopt the control layer mindset. Stop asking only which app can do a task. Start asking how the business sees, decides, protects, and learns.

The control room should lead to action

Visibility without action becomes theater. A leader can have beautiful dashboards, detailed reports, and weekly meetings full of impressive language, but if nothing changes, the business does not have a control room. It has a viewing room.

The control room has to create movement.

When a signal appears, someone should know what to do. When a risk rises, someone should own the response. When a customer issue repeats, the business should not simply count it again next week. When cash gets tight, the leader should not wait for panic. When a security concern appears, it should not sit in a vague category called 'later.'

This is where many businesses discover the real weakness. The problem was not that they lacked information. The problem was that information had no assigned owner. Nobody knew who was supposed to act. Nobody knew what level of urgency mattered. Nobody knew when to escalate. Nobody knew whether the issue had been resolved or merely discussed.

A modern control room ties information to ownership. It helps the business move from awareness to response. That is the difference between a company that watches problems and a company that leads through them.

Build the room before the storm

The worst time to build a control room is during a crisis.

When the customer is already angry, when the payment is already late, when the system is already down, when the account is already compromised, when the employee is already burned out, or when the public mistake is already spreading, the business has very little room for thoughtful design.

The companies that handle pressure better are not always the companies with the most money. They are often the companies that built visibility before they needed it.

That kind of preparation is not glamorous, but it is powerful. It is what separates businesses that survive through adrenaline from businesses that operate through discipline. The AI era will reward the disciplined business.

Seeing is only the beginning

The modern business control room is not about becoming cold, mechanical, or overly corporate. It is about giving leadership the one thing it cannot afford to lose: sight.

When a leader can see clearly, she can decide sooner. When she can decide sooner, the team can act with less confusion. When the team acts with less confusion, customers feel the difference. When customers feel the difference, trust grows.

A business that sees its own reality is harder to surprise. It is harder to manipulate. It is harder to overwhelm. It can use AI more responsibly because AI is not floating around in chaos. It is connected to a structure that already knows what matters.

This is the heart of the control room idea. Not more noise. Not more reports. Not more screens. More truth, sooner, with clearer ownership.

The next chapter takes us into the next challenge. Once the business can see more clearly, it has to decide faster. And when decisions begin moving at machine speed, leadership has to become sharper than ever.

Part Two - How the System Works Now

Chapter 8

Decisions at Machine Speed

The AI era does not only change how fast work gets done. It changes how fast decisions arrive.

That may sound small until you live inside it.

A customer sends a message and expects an answer almost immediately. A competitor launches an offer before your team has finished discussing the last one. A platform changes an algorithm and suddenly the thing that worked yesterday stops working today. A vendor updates its pricing. A review appears online. A security alert lands in the inbox. A team member needs approval. A client wants a revised proposal. A payment fails. A campaign needs to be adjusted. The business does not politely wait for a meeting next Tuesday.

This is what machine speed feels like in real life. It does not always look like robots, code, or futuristic offices. Most of the time, it looks like a human being staring at a screen with too many tabs open, trying to make a good decision while the business keeps moving underneath her feet.

And that is where many leaders misunderstand the problem. They think the pressure is coming from the amount of work. The deeper pressure is coming from the amount of decisions hidden inside the work.

Every email asks for a decision. Every delay asks for a decision. Every invoice, refund, customer complaint, software alert, employee question, marketing message, and operational exception asks for a decision. Some decisions are tiny. Some are expensive. Some are emotional. Some are risky. Some should be automated. Some should never be automated. The difficulty is knowing the difference before the pace of the business makes the choice for you.

That is why Chapter 8 matters. Once AI becomes part of the operating layer, the winning business is not simply the business that moves faster. It is the business that can decide faster without becoming reckless.

Speed is not the same thing as wisdom

There is a dangerous temptation in the AI era to confuse speed with intelligence.

A tool can generate an answer in seconds, so the answer feels impressive. A dashboard can update instantly, so the information feels urgent. An automation can move work from one place to another without asking for help, so the motion feels like progress. But speed by itself does not guarantee that the decision is good. It only guarantees that the decision happened quickly.

This distinction is going to separate strong leaders from overwhelmed leaders.

A fast bad decision is still a bad decision. In fact, it is worse than it used to be because technology can multiply the damage. A poorly written message can go out to thousands of people. A weak approval process can release incorrect information. A rushed automation can trigger the wrong workflow. A team that does not understand the data can make confident decisions from numbers that are incomplete, outdated, or misunderstood.

The old business world gave leaders more time to recover from confusion. Not always, but more often. A mistake could move slowly enough for someone to notice it before it reached every corner of the company. In a machine-speed environment, confusion travels faster. So does carelessness. So does trust.

That is why the goal is not to become the fastest person in the room. The goal is to build a business where better decisions can happen sooner because the right information, rules, people, and review points are already in place.

Machine speed rewards preparation. It punishes improvisation.

The old decision cycle is breaking

For a long time, many businesses made decisions in a rhythm that felt normal. Something happened. Someone noticed. Information was gathered. A meeting was scheduled. People discussed it. Someone followed up. A decision was made. Then the team acted.

That rhythm may still work for big strategic decisions. It may still be appropriate for hiring, partnerships, finances, legal exposure, brand direction, security policy, and anything that deserves careful human judgment. I am not suggesting every decision should be rushed through a machine.

But the daily operating rhythm has changed.

Customers are not waiting for the next meeting. Markets are not waiting for the next meeting. Cyber risks are not waiting for the next meeting. Employees working inside scattered tools are not waiting for the next meeting. The business is producing signals all day long, and those signals are asking, in one form or another, what should happen next?

This is where the old cycle starts to break. By the time a team gathers the information, the condition may have already changed. By the time an owner gets a summary, the customer may have already left. By the time a leader hears about a recurring issue, the pattern may have already cost money, reputation, or momentum.

The answer is not to panic. The answer is to redesign the decision cycle.

In the AI era, the healthier cycle looks more like this: the business detects a signal, sorts its importance, routes it to the right place, applies known rules, asks for human approval when judgment is required, takes action, records what happened, and learns from the outcome.

That may sound technical, but it is really common sense with discipline around it. A good restaurant does this. A good hospital does this. A good airport does this. A good security team does this. They do not treat every signal the same. They know what can be handled automatically, what can be escalated, what must be verified, and what requires a human being to stop and think.

Modern businesses need the same maturity, even if they are small.

A decision system beats a heroic leader

Many business owners are praised for being quick on their feet. And let me be clear: that instinct matters. There are moments when leadership requires courage, speed, and the ability to make a call without having perfect information.

But a business should not depend on the owner being heroic every day.

When every decision has to pass through one person, that person becomes the bottleneck. At first, it can feel powerful. The owner knows everything. The owner approves everything. The owner catches mistakes. The owner keeps the quality high. But over time, the same strength becomes a trap.

The business cannot move unless the owner responds. The team waits. Customers wait. Vendors wait. Opportunities wait. Then the owner gets exhausted, and the exhaustion starts making decisions too.

A decision system protects the leader from that trap.

It does not remove the leader. It supports the leader. It gives the business clear rules for what happens when common situations arise. It defines which decisions the team can make without permission, which decisions need review, which decisions should trigger an alert, and which decisions should stop until the owner or leadership team steps in.

This is not about making the business cold. It is about making the business dependable.

When the rules are clear, people feel safer. Customers get more consistent service. Employees stop guessing what the owner would want. The owner stops carrying every tiny judgment in her nervous system. AI and automation become more useful because they are operating inside boundaries instead of running wild.

That is the difference between a business that uses AI and a business that is ready for AI.

The first question is not can we automate it

One of the most important questions a leader can ask in this era is not, can we automate this?

The better question is, what kind of decision is this?

Some decisions are repetitive and low risk. They follow a pattern. They do not require deep judgment. They can often be supported or handled by automation once the rules are clear. Scheduling reminders, sorting routine messages, organizing receipts, tagging customer inquiries, drafting first-pass responses, summarizing meeting notes, flagging overdue tasks, and preparing basic reports may fall into this category.

Other decisions are judgment-heavy. They involve relationships, money, legal exposure, security, reputation, employee trust, customer promises, or ethical boundaries. These decisions may be supported by AI, but they should not be surrendered to AI.

That line matters.

AI can help gather context. It can summarize. It can compare. It can draft. It can surface patterns. It can remind the team of policy. It can help the leader see what she might have missed. But when the decision carries real responsibility, the human being must remain in control.

This is where strong businesses will develop a new kind of discipline. They will stop asking whether AI can do something and start asking whether AI should have authority to do it.

Authority is different from ability. A system may be able to send a refund, approve a discount, escalate a complaint, modify a customer record, contact a prospect, flag an employee, or lock an account. That does not mean it should be allowed to do those things without boundaries, audit trails, and human oversight where needed.

A mature business does not hand out authority casually, whether the actor is a person or a machine.

The machine-speed decision loop

The businesses that thrive in the AI era will learn to think in loops.

A loop is different from a task. A task starts and ends. A loop keeps improving. The business sees something, makes sense of it, acts on it, checks the result, and adjusts. Then it does that again. Over time, the organization becomes sharper because it is not just moving faster. It is learning faster.

This is especially powerful for small businesses because small businesses often do not lack intelligence. They lack feedback. They make decisions from fragments. One person knows what customers are saying. Another person knows what sales are doing. Another person knows what the software is showing. Another person knows what invoices are late. But the business does not bring those truths together quickly enough to make the next decision better.

An AI-ready operating layer changes that by helping the business collect signals, organize them, and turn them into usable judgment. Not perfect judgment. Usable judgment. There is a difference.

Perfect information is rarely available. Usable information is what helps you make the next responsible move. That might mean noticing that customers keep asking the same question before they buy. It might mean seeing that one service package creates more support problems than profit. It might mean realizing that a team member is constantly waiting on approvals that should have been pre-decided. It might mean identifying a recurring security weakness before it becomes a crisis.

This is why machine speed is not only about moving faster than competitors. It is about shortening the distance between signal and learning.

The shorter that distance becomes, the more responsive the business becomes.

The faster the business moves, the more important its values become. Values are not wall art in this environment. They are decision infrastructure. They tell the system where speed is helpful, where trust is more important, and where a human being must pause before the business acts.

When building systems, assume every decision leaves a trail

This is one of the reasons I think about business through a security lens.

In a serious system, a decision should not disappear into the air. If something important happens, the business should be able to answer basic questions. What triggered it? Who approved it? What information was used? What changed? When did it happen? What was the result?

Those questions are not only for giant corporations. They are for any business that wants to grow without becoming fragile.

When I think about AI and business operations, I do not only think about what the system can do. I think about what the system is allowed to do, what it records, how it can be reviewed, and how a person can step in when something does not look right. That mindset matters whether you are designing a cybersecurity platform, managing client work, running a professional service, operating a retail business, or building a team.

The audit trail is not there to make the business feel complicated. It is there to protect trust.

If a customer asks why something happened, the business should not have to shrug. If an employee makes a mistake, the business should not have to guess where the process failed. If an automation takes an action, the business should know why. If a leader needs to reverse a decision, the path should be visible.

Machine speed without memory is dangerous. The business moves, but no one can explain the movement.

Machine speed with a decision trail is different. It creates accountability. It creates learning. It gives the business a way to improve without pretending mistakes will never happen.

The real advantage is decision confidence

At the end of the day, the greatest advantage is not speed alone. It is confidence.

Confidence does not mean arrogance. It does not mean guessing loudly. It means the leader can look at the business and say, I know where the signal came from. I know what rule applied. I know when a person needs to review this. I know what we are trying to protect. I know how to learn from what happens next.

That kind of confidence changes the feel of a business.

The team becomes less reactive. The owner becomes less scattered. Customers experience more consistency. Systems become less mysterious. AI becomes less intimidating because it is no longer floating around as a shiny object. It has a job. It has boundaries. It has supervision. It has a place inside the larger operating rhythm.

This is how businesses begin to mature in the AI era. Not by pretending every decision is urgent. Not by handing the steering wheel to software. Not by slowing everything down until they miss the moment. They mature by knowing which decisions need speed, which need judgment, which need a record, and which need a human hand on the door before it opens.

The invisible war is often won or lost right there. In the moment between signal and response. In the space where a business either reacts from pressure or responds from design.

The businesses that survive will not be the ones that make every decision perfectly. No business can do that. They will be the ones that build systems capable of making better decisions sooner, learning from them faster, and protecting trust while the world keeps accelerating.

That brings us to the next place AI is changing business: the customer journey. Because when decisions move at machine speed inside the company, customers begin to feel the difference outside the company. The question is whether they feel clarity, care, and confidence, or whether they feel like they are being processed by a machine that never learned how to listen.

Chapter 9

The New Customer Journey

The customer journey used to be easier to picture.

A person saw an ad, walked into a store, picked up a brochure, called the office, asked a few questions, and eventually made a decision. Even when the process was more complicated than that, it still felt like a path. The business could imagine where the customer started, where the customer paused, and where the customer finally said yes or no.

That picture is gone.

Today, by the time a customer reaches you, they may have already been influenced by a search engine, a social media comment, a video, a review, a competitor, an AI summary, a friend's text message, a chatbot, a podcast clip, a marketplace ranking, and a feeling they cannot fully explain. They may know more than you think they know. They may also be more confused than they look. They may have compared your business against five others before you ever knew they existed.

That is the new customer journey. It is not a straight line. It is not a neat funnel. It is a web of impressions, questions, signals, doubts, and expectations moving faster than most businesses were designed to handle.

And in the AI era, the customer is not only asking, 'Can this business help me?' The customer is also asking, 'Can I trust this business to keep up with me?'

That question changes everything.

The customer arrives before they arrive

One of the biggest shifts in modern business is that the first real interaction often happens without you.

A customer may form an opinion about your company before they call, before they book, before they fill out a form, before they send a message, and before anyone on your team has a chance to make a first impression. In many cases, the first impression is not made by a human being. It is made by your website, your reviews, your response time, your social presence, your payment process, your scheduling link, your automated email, or the way your business appears in search.

That is why AI and modern systems matter. Not because they replace the human relationship, but because they protect the relationship before it starts. They help the business show up clearly when the owner is sleeping, serving another customer, driving to an appointment, coding a product, managing payroll, or trying to solve one of the hundred problems that never make it to Instagram.

The new journey begins in the invisible space. It begins in the moment the customer wonders whether a business like yours can be trusted. The business that understands this will not treat the website, inbox, calendar, review profile, CRM, and customer service system as separate pieces. It will treat them as one front door.

The journey is no longer a funnel

For years, businesses were taught to think in funnels. Awareness at the top. Interest in the middle. Purchase at the bottom. There is still value in that model, but it is no longer enough to explain how people actually move.

Customers loop. They pause. They disappear and come back. They put something in a cart and then ask a friend. They schedule a call and then read one negative review. They follow your company for months before they buy. They buy once and then judge you harder after the purchase than before it. They may not move from awareness to decision in a straight line. They may move from trust to doubt to curiosity to comparison to urgency to silence and back again.

This is not because customers are difficult. It is because customers are overloaded. They are living in the same noisy environment as the business. They have more options, more information, more warnings, more scams, more fake experts, more ads, more promises, and less patience for confusion.

So the real job of the modern business is not to shove people through a funnel. The real job is to reduce friction and increase confidence at every point where doubt can enter.

AI can help with that, but only if the business knows what it is trying to protect. If AI is used only to blast more messages, generate more content, or chase people harder, it becomes noise. But if AI is used to answer faster, organize better, personalize responsibly, track follow-up, notice patterns, summarize needs, and help the team serve with consistency, it becomes part of the trust system.

Response time is now part of the brand

There was a time when a slow reply was normal. A person left a voicemail. A business called back when it could. A customer sent an email and waited. A proposal took several days. A follow-up came next week. People did not always love the delay, but they expected it.

That expectation has changed.

The modern customer is trained by the fastest companies in the world. They may not say it out loud, but their nervous system has been shaped by same-day delivery, instant confirmations, live tracking, recommendation engines, mobile banking, streaming platforms, and apps that remember what they like. Then they come to a small business, a local service provider, a consultant, a nonprofit, a medical office, a construction company, a legal practice, a beauty brand, or a coaching business and wonder why everything feels slower.

This does not mean every business must become Amazon. That is not realistic, and it is not always desirable. But it does mean response time is no longer only an operational detail. It is part of how the customer evaluates competence.

A fast response says, 'We see you.' A clear response says, 'We understand you.' A consistent response says, 'We can be trusted.' When those three things work together, the customer relaxes. When they do not, the customer starts looking for hidden risk.

AI can support this beautifully when it is used with boundaries. It can acknowledge inquiries, route messages, summarize customer history, draft helpful replies, remind the team of open loops, identify urgent issues, and make sure no one falls through the cracks. But it should not pretend to care. It should not fake intimacy. It should not trap people in endless automation when a real human is needed.

The best customer experience in the AI era is not robotic. It is responsive, organized, and human at the right moment.

Personalization has to earn trust

Customers like being remembered. They do not like being watched.

That is one of the most important lines modern businesses need to understand. There is a difference between personalization that feels helpful and personalization that feels invasive. A business that remembers a customer's previous order, preferred appointment time, company size, skin sensitivity, project deadline, or billing preference can make the experience feel smooth. A business that overuses personal data, makes assumptions, or appears to know too much too soon can make the same customer uncomfortable.

AI makes this line even more important because it gives businesses the ability to personalize at scale. That sounds powerful, and it is. But power without judgment becomes creepy very quickly.

In the old world, personalization was often a luxury. In the new world, responsible personalization is part of professionalism.

The back office is part of the customer experience

Many business owners separate the customer experience from the back office. They imagine the customer experience as the greeting, the sales call, the service, the product, the checkout, or the thank-you message. The back office is viewed as internal. It is where the messy stuff lives: invoices, notes, scheduling, inventory, team messages, contracts, payroll, receipts, permissions, fulfillment, and follow-up.

But customers feel the back office whether they see it or not.

They feel it when an invoice is wrong. They feel it when two team members give different answers. They feel it when the business forgets a detail they already shared. They feel it when the appointment is double-booked. They feel it when the refund process is unclear. They feel it when the proposal does not match the conversation. They feel it when the company sounds warm on the front end but chaotic after payment.

This is why the AI era rewards operational maturity. Not because every business needs complicated technology, but because every business needs one version of the truth. When customer information is scattered across email, texts, spreadsheets, sticky notes, inboxes, apps, and memory, the customer eventually pays the price. They may not know why the experience feels inconsistent, but they feel it.

A modern business has to connect the promise it makes with the system that delivers the promise. That connection is where trust is either strengthened or lost.

After the sale is where the truth shows up

The sale is not the finish line. In many businesses, the sale is where the real customer journey begins.

Before someone buys, hope is doing part of the work. The customer hopes the product will help. The client hopes the service will be worth it. The patient hopes the office will be competent. The homeowner hopes the contractor will be reliable. The business owner hopes the consultant understands the pressure. The buyer hopes the company is as good as it looked online.

After the sale, hope starts asking for evidence.

Did the confirmation arrive? Did the next step make sense? Did the company remember the details? Did the product ship when promised? Did the service match the pitch? Did support respond when something went wrong? Did the business handle a mistake with honesty? Did the customer feel important after the money changed hands, or only before?

This is where AI can either become a trust builder or a trust breaker. A business can use AI to keep promises visible, follow up at the right time, check satisfaction, detect unresolved issues, and make the post-sale experience feel cared for. Or a business can use AI to send generic messages that pretend the relationship is deeper than it is.

That question should sit inside every AI decision a business makes.

The new journey requires a new kind of leadership

The customer journey is no longer owned by marketing. It is not owned by sales. It is not owned by customer service. It is not owned by operations. It belongs to the whole business.

That means leadership has to change. A leader can no longer afford to only ask, 'How do we get more leads?' That question matters, but it is too small by itself. The better question is, 'What happens to trust from the moment a person first notices us to the moment they decide whether to come back?'

That question forces a business to look at the full experience. It exposes the gaps between promise and delivery. It reveals the moments where people wait too long, repeat themselves too often, receive unclear answers, or feel like the business is making them do the work. It also reveals opportunities. A small improvement in clarity can increase trust. A better intake process can reduce stress. A faster follow-up can save a sale. A cleaner handoff can prevent a complaint. A better record of customer history can make the business feel much more personal without becoming intrusive.

That is a very different mindset from the old customer journey. It is calmer. It is wiser. It is more strategic. It also makes the business much harder to compete with because the experience is not dependent on one heroic employee remembering everything. The experience is supported by the way the business is built.

The business that feels organized wins

Customers do not need perfection. Most people are more forgiving than businesses realize. They can handle a mistake if the company owns it. They can handle a delay if the communication is honest. They can handle a policy if the policy is clear. They can handle technology if it makes the experience easier instead of colder.

What customers struggle to forgive is confusion that feels careless.

They struggle when they have to chase answers. They struggle when no one knows what was promised. They struggle when the business sounds polished before payment and scattered after payment. They struggle when every interaction feels like starting over.

The new customer journey rewards businesses that feel organized. Not stiff. Not robotic. Organized. There is a difference. An organized business can be warm. It can be bubbly. It can be deeply human. In fact, organization gives warmth somewhere to land. It allows kindness to become consistent instead of random.

That is one of the great opportunities of this era. AI can help businesses create experiences that used to require huge teams. A small company can respond with more clarity. A founder can see patterns sooner. A team can remember more. A customer can move through the process with fewer gaps. A business can become easier to trust because it becomes easier to understand.

But the technology is not the point. The point is the relationship.

The customer journey has changed because the customer has changed. People are moving through a faster, noisier, more suspicious world. They want convenience, but they also want proof. They want speed, but they also want care. They want personalization, but they also want boundaries. They want automation when it helps, and they want a human when it matters.

The businesses that win the AI era will not be the ones that automate the most. They will be the ones that use AI to make trust easier to experience.

That is the new customer journey. It begins before the customer reaches you. It continues long after the sale. And every step along the way is asking the same quiet question: can this business be trusted with my time, my money, my information, and my expectations?

The answer is no longer found in a slogan. It is found in the system behind the experience.

Chapter 10

Data: The Fuel, the Risk, and the Responsibility

Every business has a memory.

For a long time, that memory lived in ordinary places. It lived in file cabinets, notebooks, receipts, invoices, calendars, conversations, email threads, old proposals, customer notes, employee folders, bank statements, inventory sheets, and the owner's head. It was not always pretty, but it worked well enough when business moved at human speed.

You could remember the regular customer. You could look through a folder. You could call someone and ask what happened. You could flip back through a notebook or search an inbox. The system was imperfect, but the pace of business gave people room to recover.

AI changes that.

In the AI era, the memory of the business becomes one of its most important assets. Not because data sounds impressive, and not because every owner suddenly needs to talk like a Silicon Valley engineer. Data matters because it is the raw material modern systems use to understand what is happening, what happened before, what is likely to happen next, and what needs attention now.

That is powerful. It is also where many businesses get themselves into trouble. They want AI to make better decisions, but their information is scattered. They want automation to save time, but their records are messy. They want personalization, but they have not decided what should be collected, who should see it, or how it should be protected.

This is why data is not just fuel. It is also risk. And in a serious business, it becomes responsibility.

Data is not just numbers

When people hear the word data, many immediately think of spreadsheets, charts, dashboards, and complicated reports. That is part of it, but it is not the whole picture.

Data is a customer's phone number. It is a signed contract. It is a payment history. It is a text message confirming a delivery time. It is the note that says a client prefers afternoon appointments. It is the record of who changed an invoice. It is the time stamp on a refund. It is the inventory count, the lead source, the employee role, the access permission, the sales call summary, the receipt photo, the payroll file, and the password reset.

In other words, data is the evidence of how the business lives.

That is why treating data casually is dangerous. A business that handles data casually is not only risking a technical problem. It is risking trust, accuracy, money, reputation, and the ability to know what is true when pressure hits.

This matters for the average business owner because data problems often hide behind daily chaos. A customer asks for an update, and the information is in three places. A team member leaves, and no one knows what files they touched. A client complains, and the owner has to reconstruct the story from memory. At first, that does not feel like a data issue. It feels like stress.

But underneath the stress is the same problem: the business does not have a reliable memory.

AI needs clean truth

AI can move fast, but it does not magically know your business. It learns from what you give it, what you connect it to, what you ask it to analyze, and what rules you place around it.

This is where people sometimes misunderstand AI. They imagine it as a genius employee who walks in on Monday morning, understands the whole company by Tuesday, fixes the messy back office by Wednesday, and sends everyone home early by Friday. That is a lovely fantasy. It is not how serious implementation works.

AI does not eliminate the need for truth. It increases the need for truth.

If your customer records are outdated, AI may personalize based on information that is no longer accurate. If your pricing is inconsistent, AI may quote the wrong number. If your policies are buried in old documents, AI may surface the wrong version. If the system cannot tell the difference between a draft, a final agreement, and an expired document, speed becomes a liability.

That does not mean a business has to be perfect before it uses AI. If perfection were required, no one would start. But it does mean the business has to become honest about the quality of its information. AI can organize, summarize, find patterns, and reduce manual work. But when the underlying information is weak, AI does not make the business smarter. It makes the weakness louder.

The strongest businesses in this era will not simply have more data. They will have cleaner truth.

Messy data creates expensive confusion

Most data problems do not announce themselves dramatically. They creep in quietly.

A customer enters their name one way on a form and another way in the payment system. A team member saves a proposal to the wrong folder. A manager tracks a process in a private spreadsheet because the main system feels too slow. Someone copies customer details into a personal note-taking app because it is convenient. The business changes a policy but forgets to update the automation. Old permissions stay active after an employee leaves.

Individually, each one looks small. Together, they become drag.

This is the kind of drag that makes leaders feel like they are working hard but not gaining ground. The business keeps moving, but every decision requires extra checking. Every customer issue requires detective work. Every report comes with a little hesitation. Every handoff depends on someone remembering the missing piece.

In a slow environment, that drag is frustrating. In an AI environment, it becomes dangerous because automation can repeat the mistake at scale. One wrong field can affect hundreds of messages. One outdated policy can be used in dozens of conversations. One permission error can expose information to people who should not have it.

This is why operational discipline matters. It is not about making the business feel corporate or cold. It is about making sure the right information is in the right place, under the right control, at the right time.

That kind of discipline protects the warmth of the business. It gives people the confidence to move quickly without constantly wondering what they missed.

The customer is trusting you with more than a sale

When a customer gives you information, they are giving you a piece of their life.

Sometimes that information is simple. A name. An email address. A delivery preference. A billing address. Sometimes it is sensitive. A financial detail. A health concern. A home address. A legal document. A business plan. A family situation. A payroll record. A private message sent in a moment of frustration or fear.

The customer may not use the language of data governance. They may never ask about retention policies, access controls, encryption, audit logs, or vendor risk. But they absolutely know how it feels when a business is careless. They know how it feels when they get the wrong message, when their information is exposed, when a company asks for the same thing over and over, or when a private detail is handled casually.

In the AI era, customers will become more sensitive to this. They may not understand every technical detail, but they will understand the feeling of being watched, profiled, ignored, or mishandled. They will also understand the feeling of being served with care.

That is the line every modern business has to respect. Use information to make the experience better. Do not use information to manipulate people, pressure people, or pretend the relationship is deeper than it is.

Responsible data use is not only a compliance issue. It is part of the brand. It tells the customer whether the business has enough maturity to be trusted with more.

Privacy is now part of operations

In the old model, privacy often lived somewhere in the fine print. It was a link at the bottom of the website. It was a policy no one read unless something went wrong.

That approach is not enough anymore.

Privacy now lives inside daily operations. It lives in the CRM, the calendar, the payment processor, shared drives, internal chat, mobile devices, AI tools, customer portals, vendor platforms, and every automation that moves information from one place to another. Every time the business collects, stores, transfers, analyzes, or deletes information, it is making a privacy decision whether it calls it that or not.

This does not mean every small business needs a department full of lawyers. It means every serious business needs a clear sense of boundaries. What do we collect? Why do we collect it? Who can access it? What should AI be allowed to see? What should never be copied into a public tool? What should be deleted when it is no longer needed? What should be logged so we can prove what happened later?

Those are not paranoid questions. They are mature questions.

The more AI becomes part of the business, the more important those questions become. AI systems can summarize information beautifully, but they can also expose information carelessly if the business has not placed limits around them. The business that takes privacy seriously is not slowing itself down. It is building the guardrails that allow speed to become safe.

One version of the truth

A modern business cannot run well when every department has its own reality.

Sales thinks the customer bought one thing. Operations thinks the customer bought another. Finance has a different number. Customer service has a different timeline. The owner has the real story in their head, but they are on another call. The customer is waiting while the business tries to figure out itself.

This is where the idea of one version of the truth becomes practical. It does not mean one giant complicated system that controls everything. It means the business has a trusted source for important information and a disciplined way of keeping that source current.

For a small business, that might begin with clean customer records, clear file naming, shared notes, standard intake, consistent categories, and controlled access. For a growing company, it may involve integrated systems, dashboards, approval workflows, audit trails, and stronger security. The level changes with the size and risk of the business, but the principle stays the same. Important decisions should not be built on scattered memory.

AI becomes much more useful when the business has one version of the truth. It can summarize the customer relationship, identify open loops, help leadership see patterns, draft follow-ups based on accurate history, and help the team understand what matters before they walk into a meeting. But the system has to know which information is trustworthy.

This is also where leadership has to be honest. Sometimes the reason the business has messy data is not the software. It is the habits. People create side systems because the main process is unclear. They avoid updating records because the workflow is painful. They keep information to themselves because sharing has never been rewarded. Better data begins with better behavior.

Ownership matters

One of the most dangerous phrases in business is "someone should handle that."

Someone should clean the records. Someone should update the policy. Someone should remove old access. Someone should check whether the AI tool is allowed to process that information. Someone should make sure the customer file is complete. Someone should know where the final contract lives.

When everyone assumes someone is responsible, the business quietly creates a gap. And in the AI era, gaps get expensive.

Data needs ownership. Not in a complicated, intimidating way, but in a clear way. The business needs to know who is responsible for the accuracy of important information, who approves changes, who can access sensitive records, who reviews exceptions, and who notices when the system starts drifting.

Clear ownership also protects the leader. Too many founders carry the whole company in their head because the business never built a memory outside of them. That may work in the early days, but eventually it becomes a ceiling. The business can only move as fast as the person everyone has to ask.

A stronger business distributes memory without losing control. It gives the team access to what they need, protects what they do not need, and keeps a record of what changed. That is not cold. That is how trust survives growth.

The fuel, the risk, and the responsibility

Data is the fuel because it gives AI something to work with. Without it, the system is guessing from the outside.

Data is the risk because information can be wrong, exposed, misused, misunderstood, or carried into places it should never go.

Data is the responsibility because customers, employees, vendors, partners, and communities are trusting the business to handle pieces of their lives with care.

A business that understands all three will approach AI differently. It will not rush to connect every tool to every file. It will not confuse access with intelligence. It will not treat customer information as free raw material. It will build a cleaner memory, stronger boundaries, and better habits before asking AI to move faster on its behalf.

That may sound slower at first, but it is actually the faster path. Clean truth reduces rework. Clear ownership reduces confusion. Good boundaries reduce damage. Better records reduce stress. Responsible systems allow the business to scale without constantly stepping on its own shoelaces.

This is the part of AI that does not always make the exciting headline. It is not the shiny demonstration, the viral prompt, or the futuristic promise. It is the foundation underneath all of it.

And that brings us to the next danger.

Once people see what AI can do, it becomes very easy to believe the hype. It becomes easy to mistake motion for progress, automation for strategy, and a clever demo for a real business advantage.

That is where many companies will lose money, time, trust, and focus.

Because in the invisible war for the future of business, the enemy is not only moving too slowly. Sometimes the enemy is chasing the wrong thing too fast.

Part Three - The Threats

Chapter 11

The Hype Trap

Hype is what happens when excitement outruns judgment.

Every era of business has its own version of it. A new platform appears. A new strategy becomes fashionable. A new expert says the old rules are dead. A new tool promises to save time, increase revenue, reduce staff burden, transform customer experience, and make the business look modern before anyone has asked whether the business actually needs it.

AI has brought the loudest version of that pattern most owners have ever seen.

One day, artificial intelligence sounded like something that belonged to research labs, giant technology companies, or science fiction movies. Then almost overnight, it became the thing everyone was supposed to understand, buy, use, and explain. Leaders started hearing that AI would rewrite industries. Employees started testing tools quietly. Vendors started adding AI to every product page. Social media filled with screenshots, prompts, productivity tricks, and bold claims about what one person could now do in a day.

Some of the excitement is justified. AI is powerful. It can help a business move faster, see patterns, reduce repetitive work, improve customer response, support decision-making, and give smaller teams leverage they did not have before.

But excitement is not strategy.

A business can be impressed by AI and still be disciplined. It can be optimistic without being careless. It can adopt new tools without surrendering its common sense. The danger is not that leaders will believe AI matters. The danger is that they will believe every AI claim matters equally.

Hype is pressure dressed up as opportunity

The hype trap rarely feels like a trap at first. It usually feels like urgency.

The owner hears that competitors are using AI. The team sees other companies posting about automation. A vendor says the new feature is essential. A consultant warns that slow adopters will be left behind. A headline suggests that entire jobs are changing. A customer expects a faster response. Suddenly, the leader is not making a calm decision about the business. The leader is trying not to feel late.

That emotional pressure matters because rushed adoption creates sloppy adoption. When a business buys from fear, it often skips the questions that would have protected it. What problem are we solving? What process will this improve? What information does the tool need? Who will review the output? What happens if it is wrong? What data leaves our control? How will we know whether this actually made the business stronger?

Those questions are not meant to slow innovation. They are what keep innovation from becoming another expensive distraction.

Hype tells the owner, "You need this now." Leadership asks, "For what, exactly?"

That small pause is where wisdom enters the room.

The demo is not the business

One of the reasons AI hype spreads so quickly is that AI demos beautifully.

A tool can draft a message in seconds. It can summarize a document. It can generate an image, outline a proposal, answer a customer question, organize notes, or create a plan that looks polished. The first time someone sees that happen, the reaction is real. It feels like the future has walked through the front door and sat down at the desk.

But a demo is not the same thing as a durable business advantage.

A demo shows what a tool can do in a controlled moment. A business has to know what the tool will do on a tired Tuesday, with incomplete information, under pressure, with a customer waiting, with an employee making assumptions, with old data in the system, with a refund on the line, with a vendor contract involved, and with someone needing to prove what happened later.

That is where the real test begins.

Many AI tools can produce impressive output. Fewer can fit responsibly into a real operating system. The business has to think about workflow, ownership, security, review, accuracy, permission, and accountability. If no one knows where the output goes, who approved it, what source it used, or whether it should have touched that data in the first place, the business did not gain intelligence. It gained theater.

The serious leader learns to admire the demo without being seduced by it.

Shiny tools can hide weak systems

The easiest mistake in the AI era is believing that a new tool will fix an old disorder.

A scattered business may buy an AI assistant and still have scattered customer records. A slow business may automate a broken process and make the broken process move faster. A team with unclear roles may add AI and create more confusion about who owns the final decision. A company with weak security may connect sensitive files to a tool without understanding where the information goes.

This is why AI does not automatically modernize a business. It magnifies the quality of the system it enters.

If the system is disciplined, AI can add speed. If the system is messy, AI can add noise. If the business has clear standards, AI can help people follow them. If the standards are vague, AI may make the vagueness sound confident.

That last part is especially dangerous because AI can make weak thinking look polished. A vague plan can become a beautiful document. A shallow strategy can become a convincing presentation. A wrong answer can sound calm and professional. A risky shortcut can appear efficient because it is formatted neatly.

Polish is not proof.

In the old workday, confusion often looked like piles of paper, long email threads, and people asking the same question over and over. In the AI era, confusion may look much cleaner. It may arrive as a well-written summary, a sleek dashboard, a generated report, or an automated message that no human fully reviewed.

That is why leaders need more judgment, not less.

Buying relief is not the same as building capability

A lot of AI purchases begin with a very human feeling: relief.

The owner is tired of repetitive work. The team is stretched. Customers expect more. The back office is overloaded. Marketing feels endless. Hiring is hard. The inbox never stops. So when a product promises to reduce pressure, the promise feels personal.

There is nothing wrong with wanting relief. Most businesses need it. Repetitive work drains people. Manual follow-up creates mistakes. Owners should not have to spend their best thinking hours copying information from one place to another.

The problem begins when relief becomes the entire buying standard.

A tool can make something feel easier while making the business more fragile. It can reduce one task while creating a hidden dependency. It can save a few hours while introducing new data risk. It can give employees shortcuts before the business has decided what should be reviewed by a human. It can make the leader feel modern without actually improving control.

Capability is different from relief. Capability means the business becomes stronger because the system is clearer, the work is safer, the decisions are better supported, and the team knows how to operate without guessing.

The best AI adoption should give a business relief and capability. If it only gives relief, the leader should keep asking questions.

The tool should serve the operating model

The most disciplined businesses do not start with the tool. They start with the operating model.

How does this business create value? Where does information enter? Where do decisions happen? What work repeats? What work requires judgment? What must be protected? What must be visible to leadership? What should a customer feel when the system is working well?

Once those answers are clearer, AI becomes easier to place. It might belong in intake, where information is collected and organized. It might belong in customer service, where common questions can be answered faster with human escalation. It might belong in finance, where receipts, categories, reminders, and visibility matter. It might belong in operations, where tasks, follow-ups, and handoffs can be tracked. It might belong in security, where unusual activity needs attention before it becomes damage.

But the placement should be intentional. The business should not sprinkle AI over every surface and call that transformation.

Random adoption creates random responsibility. One employee uses one tool. Another employee uses a different one. A manager adds an automation. A vendor includes a feature no one understands. Customer data moves quietly through systems no one mapped. The owner thinks the business is becoming more advanced, but in reality the operating picture is getting harder to see.

The tool should serve the business. The business should not reorganize itself around every tool that arrives with a shiny promise.

Smart questions beat loud promises

There is a simple way to spot the hype trap: notice when the promise is bigger than the explanation.

If a tool says it will transform your business but cannot clearly explain what it changes, how it protects information, how output is reviewed, how errors are handled, how people stay in control, and how success is measured, the leader should not be embarrassed to slow down.

Strong businesses ask plain questions. What does this actually do? What does it need access to? Who owns the result? What happens when it is wrong? Can we turn it off? Can we audit it? Does it integrate with the way we already work? Does it make our team smarter, or does it make them dependent? Does it improve trust, or does it simply increase activity?

Those questions do not require a computer science degree. They require leadership.

This is important for average owners because the AI conversation can make people feel small. Some leaders stay quiet because they do not want to sound behind. They nod through vendor calls. They accept vague explanations. They pretend to understand more than they do because the room seems to reward confidence.

Do not do that.

A serious leader is allowed to ask simple questions until the answer becomes clear. In fact, that is often the strongest thing a leader can do. Complexity should not be used as a fog machine. If a tool is going to touch your customers, your data, your team, or your decisions, you have the right to understand it in plain language.

Disciplined curiosity is the way forward

The answer to hype is not fear. It is disciplined curiosity.

Fear says, "Do nothing until everything is safe." Hype says, "Do everything before you get left behind." Disciplined curiosity says, "Learn quickly, test carefully, measure honestly, and keep humans responsible for what matters."

That is the posture modern leaders need. They should be curious enough to experiment and disciplined enough to protect the business while they do it. They should let teams learn, but not in secret. They should test use cases, but not with sensitive data in uncontrolled tools. They should celebrate speed, but not when speed skips review. They should listen to vendors, but not outsource judgment to them.

This is where a business begins to build real AI maturity. Not by chasing every trend, and not by refusing to change, but by developing a repeatable way to decide what belongs inside the business and what does not.

A mature business can say yes with structure. It can also say no without panic.

That is powerful. In a noisy market, the ability to say no is part of competitive strength.

The Aetis lesson: control before speed

Building a security-first operating platform changes how you see technology.

When you are building something that has to protect information, support decisions, organize business operations, and create accountability, you cannot afford to be impressed by surface-level speed alone. You learn to ask what sits underneath the feature. You learn to care about permissions, audit trails, workflows, escalation, visibility, and what happens when the system is under stress.

That is one of the lessons behind the work of Aetis. The point is not simply to add more AI to business. The point is to make business more controlled, more protected, more visible, and more capable in an AI-shaped world.

That distinction matters. Anyone can chase features. Serious builders create environments where features can be used safely. Anyone can produce a fast answer. Serious operators ask whether the answer is grounded, authorized, useful, and reviewed when review is necessary.

This is the difference between looking modern and becoming resilient.

The hype trap rewards the appearance of movement. A control-first mindset rewards the quality of movement.

Do not let excitement replace judgment

AI deserves attention. It deserves study. It deserves experimentation. It deserves a real seat in the business conversation.

What it does not deserve is blind obedience.

A leader should not adopt AI because everyone is talking about it. A leader should adopt AI where it creates meaningful leverage, protects or improves trust, reduces unnecessary burden, strengthens decision-making, and fits inside an operating model the business can actually manage.

That is the difference between being current and being controlled. The goal is not to look like an AI company. The goal is to build a better business in the AI era.

Some businesses will lose themselves in hype. They will buy too many tools, automate too quickly, expose too much information, confuse activity with progress, and exhaust their teams with constant change. They will mistake the feeling of motion for the discipline of movement.

Other businesses will move differently. They will learn. They will test. They will ask sharper questions. They will build guardrails. They will protect judgment. They will use AI where it belongs and refuse it where it does not.

Those are the businesses that will earn trust while others are still chasing trends.

The invisible war is not won by the company that gets excited the fastest. It is won by the company that can stay clear while everyone else is reacting.

And that leads to the next threat.

Once a business falls in love with speed, it becomes tempting to automate more than it understands. It becomes tempting to remove human friction from places where human judgment is actually the protection.

That is how automation stops being leverage and starts becoming liability.

Chapter 12

Automation Without Judgment

Automation is powerful because it removes delay. It becomes dangerous when it removes responsibility.

That is the line every modern business has to learn to see.

In the old workday, most mistakes had friction around them. A person had to type the email, send the invoice, approve the order, update the customer record, move the file, answer the message, or make the phone call. That did not make the old way perfect. Far from it. People forgot things. They entered information wrong. They missed deadlines. They made judgment calls when they were tired, rushed, distracted, or overwhelmed.

But the old way had one hidden advantage: slowness gave people moments to notice.

Someone could pause before sending. A manager could catch an unusual request. An employee could ask, "Does this look right?" A customer could push back before the next step happened. The delay was frustrating, but sometimes the delay acted like a guardrail.

AI and automation change that. Now a message can be drafted, scheduled, personalized, routed, logged, and followed up before anyone has fully thought through whether the message should have been sent in the first place.

A workflow can move a customer from interest to payment to onboarding to renewal with very little human involvement. A finance process can categorize, flag, remind, and report. A hiring process can screen, rank, and respond. A security process can detect, block, and escalate.

That is the opportunity. It is also the risk.

Speed is not the same as wisdom

The promise of automation is seductive because every business owner understands the pain of repetition.

Nobody starts a business because they dream of chasing receipts, copying notes between systems, sending the same follow-up email for the hundredth time, reminding customers about missing forms, checking whether a task was completed, or asking the team for another update that should have been visible already.

So when automation offers to take that work away, it feels like a gift. And in many cases, it is. Repetitive work should not consume the best energy of a human team. A business that can remove unnecessary manual drag should absolutely do it.

But the leader has to separate two kinds of work that often look similar from a distance. There is repetitive work, and there is judgment work.

Repetitive work follows a known pattern. Send the confirmation. Attach the receipt. Move the task to the next stage. Remind the customer about the appointment. Pull the standard report. Organize the documents in the right folder.

Judgment work asks whether the pattern still fits. Should this customer receive the standard message? Is this charge unusual? Does this refund request deserve escalation? Is this employee behavior a training issue, a management issue, or a warning sign? Is this vendor request normal, or is someone trying to exploit the system? Is the automated answer technically correct but emotionally wrong?

Automation is excellent at repeating patterns. It is not automatically excellent at knowing when a pattern should stop.

That is why speed without wisdom can make a business look efficient while quietly making it brittle.

Bad judgment at scale is still bad judgment

One of the great misconceptions about automation is that it makes a process better simply because it makes the process faster.

It does not.

Automation multiplies whatever logic it is given. If the workflow is thoughtful, automation can multiply discipline. If the workflow is sloppy, automation can multiply confusion. If the policy is fair, automation can help apply it consistently. If the policy is vague, automation can turn vagueness into a thousand tiny decisions that no one remembers making.

Customers receive messages that are technically on schedule but wrong for the moment. Employees get tasks without context. Managers see dashboards without understanding the assumptions behind them. Owners receive reports that look clean while the actual work underneath is messy. Everyone is moving, but fewer people understand the movement.

That is not transformation. That is disorder with a faster engine.

The question is not, "Can this be automated?" In the AI era, the answer will often be yes. The better question is, "Should this be automated, under what conditions, and who is responsible when the automation acts?"

The quiet danger of invisible decisions

The most dangerous automations are not always the dramatic ones.

They are often the quiet ones. A routing rule that sends certain customers to one queue and others to another. A scoring system that decides which lead deserves attention. A billing rule that applies a fee. A template that changes the tone of a customer response. A permission setting that gives one person access and keeps another person out. A reminder sequence that keeps pushing even after the situation has changed.

Each individual action may seem small. But together, those actions shape the experience of the business. They shape who gets served quickly, who gets ignored, who gets escalated, who gets trusted, who gets questioned, and where the team spends its energy.

That is why invisible decisions deserve visible ownership.

If a business cannot explain why an automation exists, what it does, what it touches, what it assumes, who approved it, and how it can be corrected, the business has allowed a hidden decision-maker into the company. It may not feel like that because the automation is not a person. It does not have a desk. It does not speak up in a meeting. It just runs.

But anything that changes a customer outcome, an employee workload, a financial record, a security response, or a leadership decision is participating in the business.

Participation requires accountability.

Human-in-the-loop is not a slogan

You will hear the phrase human-in-the-loop often in conversations about AI. It sounds reassuring. It suggests that people are still involved, that the machine is not fully in charge, and that judgment has not been removed.

But saying a human is in the loop is not the same as designing a loop a human can actually use.

A real human-in-the-loop model must answer practical questions. Where does the human enter? What exactly are they reviewing? What information do they see? Do they have enough context to disagree? Can they override the system? Are they given time to think? Are they trained to spot the risk? Is their decision recorded? Are they punished for slowing the process down when slowing down was the responsible thing to do?

Human judgment should not be a ceremonial checkpoint. It should be a meaningful control. The person reviewing the work must have authority, context, and permission to interrupt the machine when interruption protects the business.

Automate the task, not the conscience

The strongest businesses will learn to automate confidently without becoming careless.

They will automate reminders, document collection, scheduling, status updates, routine summaries, receipt organization, simple categorization, duplicate checking, and standard information retrieval. They will use AI to reduce the burden of repetitive work so people can spend more time on relationships, strategy, creativity, service, and problem-solving.

But they will be careful around decisions that carry emotional, financial, legal, ethical, security, or reputational weight.

A customer complaint may need a human ear. A refund dispute may need context. A hiring decision may need fairness review. A payroll issue may need sensitivity. A security alert may need investigation. A public message may need tone judgment. A contract exception may need leadership approval. A vulnerable customer may need care that a template cannot provide.

This does not mean AI has no role in those moments. It may help summarize, gather evidence, suggest options, identify history, flag risk, or prepare a draft. But assistance is not the same as authority.

The business has to decide where AI may assist and where a human must decide.

That is one of the most important operating rules of the AI era.

The small-business problem

Smaller businesses usually do not have that luxury.

The owner is the strategist, the decision-maker, the problem solver, the emergency contact, the customer service backup, the financial reviewer, the hiring manager, and sometimes the person trying to figure out why the software will not connect to the other software.

That is why automation can feel especially attractive to a smaller business. It promises leverage without a large team. It promises professionalism without a department. It promises consistency without constant supervision.

Used well, that leverage is real. But the smaller the team, the more important the judgment layer becomes. There may not be a compliance department down the hall to catch a bad workflow. There may not be an IT team reviewing every integration. There may not be a legal team checking every template. The owner has to build simple, practical controls into the way the business adopts automation.

Before automating, the owner should understand the rule, the data, the action, the exception, the review point, and the person responsible. If those pieces are not clear, the business is not ready for full automation. It may be ready for AI assistance, but not for AI authority.

The Aetis lesson: every action needs a trail

When you build with security in mind, you become allergic to invisible action.

It is not enough for a system to do something. A serious system has to show what happened, when it happened, why it happened, what information was used, who authorized it, and what changed afterward. That is the difference between convenience and control.

This is one of the reasons the Aetis mindset matters in this book. The future of business is not just more automation. The future of business is accountable automation. It is work that moves faster while still leaving a trace. It is AI that assists without hiding. It is software that supports decisions instead of quietly swallowing them.

A business owner should not have to choose between speed and visibility. The best systems will provide both. They will make repetitive work lighter while making important actions more traceable. They will help teams move quickly without making leadership blind.

That is the standard modern businesses should expect.

A simple rule for responsible automation

There is a simple way to think about automation in a real business.

Automate what is repeatable. Assist what is complex. Escalate what is sensitive. Record what matters.

If the work is repeatable and low risk, automation can often handle it. If the work is complex, AI may help organize the facts, but a person should still think. If the work is sensitive, the system should escalate rather than decide alone. If the action affects money, access, customers, trust, security, or reputation, the business should keep a record that can be reviewed later.

Do not remove the pause from places that need one

Some pauses are waste. Others are protection.

The wisdom of the AI era is knowing the difference.

A pause before sending a standard appointment reminder may be unnecessary. A pause before terminating an account may be essential. A pause before categorizing a receipt may be wasteful. A pause before denying service may be responsible. A pause before updating a public page may slow the team down. A pause before issuing a public statement may protect the entire brand.

Automation invites leaders to remove friction. That is often good. But the best leaders will not remove every point of friction simply because technology makes it possible.

They will ask where friction is simply drag and where friction is judgment wearing a different coat.

The next threat

Automation without judgment is one of the fastest ways for a business to lose control while feeling productive.

The dashboard looks active. The notifications keep moving. The customer journey advances. The reports update. The team feels less manual pressure. From the outside, the business may appear more advanced.

But if no one understands the rules underneath, if no one owns the exceptions, if no one can explain the decision trail, and if no one has authority to stop the machine when the machine is wrong, the business has not become smarter. It has become dependent.

The strongest companies in the AI era will not be the ones that automate everything. They will be the ones that know what to automate, what to assist, what to review, and what to protect.

That leads directly to the next danger.

Even when a business makes thoughtful automation choices, it can still weaken itself by spreading those choices across too many disconnected tools. One tool handles customers. Another handles money. Another handles tasks. Another handles files. Another handles security. Another holds the data no one remembers to update.

At first, that looks like flexibility.

Over time, it becomes fragmentation.

Chapter 13

The Hidden Cost of Fragmented Tools

Most businesses do not become complicated on purpose. They become complicated one helpful tool at a time.

That is what makes fragmentation so easy to miss.

No owner wakes up and says, "Today I would like my customer information in one place, my invoices in another place, my files in a third place, my team conversations in a fourth place, and my security decisions somewhere no one checks unless something goes wrong." Nobody designs that kind of confusion intentionally. It usually happens because the business is growing, the owner is tired, the team needs relief, and a new tool promises to solve one immediate problem.

At first, the new tool feels like progress. The scheduling tool saves time. The payment tool makes checkout easier. The project management tool gives the team a place to track work. The marketing tool sends messages automatically. The file-sharing tool keeps documents moving. The customer system remembers names, emails, and notes. Each piece helps in its own way.

Then one day the owner looks up and realizes the business is not running on a system. It is running on a collection.

That collection may look modern from the outside, but underneath, the truth of the business is scattered. No single place knows the whole customer. No single place knows the whole financial picture. No single place knows the whole workflow. No single place knows who has access to what. No single place can explain what happened from start to finish.

That is the hidden cost of fragmented tools.

The invisible tax on every decision

Fragmentation is not just an inconvenience. It is a tax.

It taxes time because people have to look in multiple places before they can answer a simple question. It taxes attention because the mind has to switch from one screen to another, one password to another, one notification stream to another. It taxes leadership because the owner is constantly trying to assemble a full picture from partial information.

The frustrating part is that this tax rarely appears on a bill. A business owner can see the monthly price of a subscription. What they cannot always see is the cost of the minutes lost, the errors introduced, the duplicate entries created, the follow-ups missed, the customer context forgotten, or the staff energy drained by jumping between systems all day.

That hidden cost is often larger than the subscription itself.

A ten-dollar tool can become expensive if it creates twenty minutes of extra work every day. A free app can become costly if it holds information no one else can see. A cheap workaround can become dangerous if it becomes the unofficial place where important decisions live.

In the AI era, this matters even more because speed magnifies the cost of confusion. When a business moves slowly, fragmentation is annoying. When a business moves at machine speed, fragmentation becomes a liability.

AI cannot fix what the business cannot find

Many leaders assume AI will solve the fragmentation problem for them.

They imagine AI sitting above the business like a brilliant assistant, pulling everything together, understanding every customer, summarizing every task, reading every message, tracking every invoice, and keeping everyone aligned. That future is possible, but not by magic.

AI can only work with the truth it can reach.

If the customer history is split across email, a spreadsheet, a CRM, handwritten notes, old text messages, and the memory of one employee, AI does not automatically know the full story. If financial information lives in one system while receipts live in another and approvals happen in a chat thread, AI cannot reliably explain what happened without access, structure, and rules. If the team is using different tools for the same type of work, AI may summarize activity without understanding which source is authoritative.

This is where businesses can get a false sense of intelligence.

The AI may sound confident. It may produce a clean answer. It may summarize beautifully. But if the data underneath is incomplete, duplicated, outdated, or scattered, the answer may be polished and still be wrong.

That is why leaders cannot treat AI like a magic layer they pour over chaos. AI works best when it sits on top of a business that knows where its truth lives.

When the customer becomes a puzzle

The first place fragmentation usually shows itself is in the customer experience.

A customer does not care how many systems a business uses. They care whether the business remembers who they are, what they asked for, what they paid for, what was promised, what went wrong, and what needs to happen next.

When the customer journey is fragmented, the business starts asking the customer to repeat themselves. The sales conversation does not fully reach the service team. The payment record does not fully connect to the delivery record. The support issue does not connect to the original promise. The follow-up message does not reflect the last conversation. The customer may feel as if every department is meeting them for the first time.

That is not just inefficient. It damages trust.

People are more forgiving when a business is honest and organized. They are less forgiving when the business appears confused about its own commitments. Confusion makes customers nervous. It makes them wonder whether the company is paying attention. It makes them wonder whether the left hand knows what the right hand is doing.

In a world where customers expect fast, personalized, informed service, fragmented tools quietly make a business look less professional than it really is.

When the team becomes the integration

If the tools do not connect, the people become the connection.

That sentence explains a great deal of modern workplace exhaustion.

An employee copies information from one place to another. A manager screenshots a report and posts it in a chat. A coordinator updates a spreadsheet because the project tool does not match the billing tool. A team member sends a reminder because the system reminder was not trusted. Someone exports, imports, checks, rechecks, and then apologizes when the number still does not match.

The business may think it has software. In reality, it has people holding the software together with attention, memory, and manual labor.

That is not a technology strategy. That is a hidden staffing cost.

The most capable people often absorb this cost first because they are the ones who know how everything works. They remember where the exceptions live. They know which report is reliable and which report has to be adjusted. They know which customer notes are current and which ones are old. They know which tool the owner checks and which tool the team actually uses.

That knowledge makes them valuable, but it also makes the business fragile. If they are unavailable, overwhelmed, or gone, the system knowledge leaves with them.

A strong business should not depend on one person being the bridge between every disconnected tool.

The security problem hiding inside convenience

Fragmentation is also a security problem.

Every tool creates another place where data can live, another login to manage, another permission to review, another integration to monitor, another vendor to trust, and another point where a mistake can expose the business.

That does not mean every tool is bad. Modern businesses need software. The danger is not software itself. The danger is uncontrolled sprawl.

Sprawl happens when the business keeps adding tools without a clear access model. One employee gets added to a system for a temporary task and never removed. A contractor receives access to a shared folder and keeps it long after the project ends. A payment platform connects to another app, but no one remembers who approved the connection. A team member uses a personal account because it was faster than waiting for a proper setup.

These moments may seem small. In cybersecurity, small moments are often where real risk begins.

A business cannot protect what it cannot see. If leadership does not know where sensitive data lives, who can reach it, what systems are connected, and which accounts are still active, the business is trusting luck instead of governance.

In the AI era, that kind of luck is not enough.

The reporting illusion

Fragmented tools can also create the illusion of visibility.

Each platform has a dashboard. The marketing tool has reports. The sales tool has reports. The accounting tool has reports. The project tool has reports. The customer service tool has reports. At a glance, it looks like the business is surrounded by data.

But more dashboards do not always mean more clarity.

One system may define a customer one way, another system may define a customer differently. One tool may count a lead after a form submission, another after a conversation, another after a payment. One report may use gross revenue while another uses collected revenue. One platform may show completed tasks while another still shows open work connected to the same customer.

The leader then has to interpret conflicting pictures. Which number is real? Which report should be trusted? Why does one dashboard say the business is healthy while another suggests there is a problem?

This is how dashboards become decoration instead of decision support.

Real visibility requires shared definitions. Without shared definitions, a business is not looking at one truth from different angles. It is looking at different truths and hoping they mean the same thing.

Integration is not the same as alignment

A common response to fragmentation is to connect everything.

That can help, but it is not the whole answer.

An integration moves data between systems. Alignment decides what the data means, which system is the source of truth, who owns the process, what happens when information conflicts, and how exceptions are handled.

Without alignment, integrations can simply move confusion faster.

A bad field mapping can send the wrong status to the wrong place. A duplicate contact can create two versions of the same customer. A stale permission can follow someone across systems. A poorly designed automation can update records before a human has confirmed the facts. The business may feel connected, but the connection is not disciplined.

That is why the modern leader has to think beyond apps and connections. The real question is not, "Can these tools talk to each other?" The real question is, "Do they support one operating truth?"

The control layer mindset

This is where the control layer mindset becomes important.

A control layer does not mean one giant piece of software that replaces every tool overnight. It means the business has a clear way to understand the work across tools. It knows where core records live. It knows which actions matter. It knows who has authority. It knows what must be logged. It knows which data should move, which data should be protected, and which decisions require review.

In plain language, the control layer keeps the business from becoming a junk drawer.

This is the thinking behind the Aetis approach: security, operations, visibility, and accountability cannot be treated as separate conversations forever. A business that wants to operate at machine speed needs more than tools. It needs a way to see the business as one living system.

That does not mean every small business needs enterprise complexity. It means every business needs a simple architecture of truth. Who is the customer? What was promised? What was paid? What work is active? Who is responsible? Who has access? What changed? Where is the record?

Those questions are not technical. They are leadership questions.

The owner test

Here is one of the simplest tests a business owner can use.

Ask: if I needed to understand this customer, this invoice, this project, this employee access, or this decision tomorrow morning, where would I look first?

If the answer is clear, the business has a foundation. If the answer depends on who is working that day, which tool was updated last, or whether someone remembers the backstory, the business has fragmentation risk.

The strongest businesses will not be the ones with the most apps. They will be the ones with the clearest operating truth.

What fragmentation really steals

Fragmentation steals more than time.

It steals confidence. The owner hesitates because they are not sure which number is right. The team hesitates because they are not sure which instruction is current. The customer hesitates because the business seems uncertain. The leader hesitates because every decision requires a scavenger hunt.

That hesitation is expensive.

Business in the AI era rewards clarity. It rewards companies that can see, decide, act, and explain. Fragmented companies may still move, but they move with drag. They spend energy reconciling their own systems while more organized competitors spend that same energy serving customers, improving operations, and building trust.

The goal is not to chase perfection. The goal is to reduce the drag that keeps the business from operating like one business.

The next threat

Fragmented tools are dangerous because they make the business harder to see.

But there is another danger that sits right beside fragmentation. Once a business depends on tools it does not fully understand, it also depends on risks it may not know how to measure.

That is where AI and cybersecurity meet the business owner directly.

In the next chapter, we will talk about the part many leaders still try to avoid: security is no longer only an IT issue. In an AI-powered business, security is part of operations, reputation, customer trust, financial protection, and leadership responsibility.

Part Three - The Threats

Chapter 14

AI, Cybersecurity, and the Business Owner

There was a time when a business owner could hear the word cybersecurity and quietly place it in someone else's department.

That time is over.

Not because every owner needs to become a programmer, a hacker, or a network engineer. That is not realistic, and honestly, it is not the job. The owner does not need to know every technical detail hiding behind the screen. But the owner does need to understand something bigger: in the AI era, cybersecurity is not just a technology issue. It is a business issue.

It touches money. It touches customer trust. It touches contracts. It touches employee access. It touches reputation. It touches whether the business can open tomorrow morning and keep serving people without panic.

When AI enters the business, the stakes rise because the business is no longer just storing information. It is asking systems to interpret information, act on information, move information, summarize information, and sometimes make recommendations based on information. That creates power. It also creates responsibility.

A business that uses AI without thinking about security is not becoming modern. It is becoming exposed.

Security is not fear. Security is maturity.

One of the reasons business owners avoid cybersecurity is that the subject often arrives wrapped in fear.

Someone tells them about hackers, breaches, ransomware, scams, stolen passwords, fake invoices, impersonation, data leaks, and lawsuits. The owner hears all of that and thinks, "I do not have time for this. I am already trying to keep the business alive."

I understand that reaction.

Most owners are not careless. They are overloaded. They are selling, hiring, paying bills, answering customers, solving problems, managing tools, and trying to make decisions with imperfect information. When cybersecurity is presented as one more terrifying subject, it becomes easier to avoid than to face.

But strong security is not about living scared. Strong security is about building a business that can be trusted.

It is the digital version of locking the door, counting the register, checking who has keys, keeping contracts where they belong, and making sure the person handling money is the person authorized to handle money. Those are not dramatic ideas. They are basic business discipline.

AI does not change that principle. AI makes it more important.

The business is now the target

A lot of small and growing businesses still carry an old belief that danger is mostly aimed at big companies.

They imagine criminals chasing banks, hospitals, governments, giant retailers, and major technology firms. Those organizations do face serious threats, but the modern attacker is not only looking for size. They are looking for opportunity.

A smaller business may have less money, but it may also have weaker controls. It may reuse passwords. It may not remove old employee access. It may not know which vendors can reach its data. It may not have clear approval rules for payments. It may rely on one overloaded person to recognize every suspicious message. It may trust convenience over verification because the team is moving fast.

That is exactly why business owners have to pay attention.

The question is not, "Why would anyone come after us?" The better question is, "Where have we made it too easy for someone to use our own systems against us?"

That shift matters. It moves the owner from helpless fear to practical leadership.

AI creates speed. Speed creates openings.

The same thing that makes AI useful also makes it risky: speed.

AI can write faster, summarize faster, respond faster, sort faster, search faster, and make connections faster than a person working manually. That speed is why businesses want it. But speed without guardrails can turn a small mistake into a large problem before anyone has time to notice.

A poorly reviewed AI-generated message can go to a customer sounding confident but saying the wrong thing. An automation can send a file to the wrong place because no one checked the permissions. A chatbot can answer questions using outdated information. A team member can paste sensitive customer details into a tool without understanding where that data goes. An assistant can summarize a conversation and accidentally expose something that should have stayed private.

None of these examples require a villain in a hoodie. They require normal people moving fast inside systems they do not fully understand.

That is the new security reality. Some of the biggest risks are not dramatic attacks. They are ordinary workflow moments happening at machine speed.

The new version of locking the door

Every business owner understands physical security instinctively.

If you own a storefront, you do not leave the front door open overnight. If you keep cash on site, you do not let every person touch it. If you have private records, you do not stack them on the sidewalk. If an employee leaves, you do not intentionally let them keep the keys forever.

Digital business needs the same common sense, translated into modern systems.

Passwords are keys. Admin accounts are master keys. Customer records are private files. Payment platforms are registers. Shared drives are filing rooms. Automations are employees that never sleep. AI assistants are powerful helpers that need boundaries. Vendor integrations are side doors into the business.

When owners see security that way, it stops feeling like a foreign language.

The question becomes simple: who has keys, what can they open, what should they never touch, and how quickly can we know if something changes?

Trust breaks quietly before it breaks publicly

One of the hardest things about security is that damage often begins before anyone announces it.

A customer may not immediately know that their information was handled carelessly. A vendor may not immediately know that an invoice was changed. An owner may not immediately know that an old login still works. A team may not immediately know that a shared document has the wrong permission setting.

The business can look normal on the outside while trust is weakening underneath.

Then one day the problem becomes visible. A customer asks why they received a message they should not have received. A payment goes to the wrong account. A file appears where it should not. A former employee still has access. A fake message looks real enough to fool someone. A customer realizes the company does not know where their data went.

That is when trust becomes expensive to repair.

The public mistake is usually only the final moment. The real failure happened earlier, when the business did not have enough visibility, control, or verification built into the way it operated.

AI can make scams look professional

Business owners also have to understand that AI does not only help good businesses move faster. It can help dishonest people look more believable.

A scam message no longer has to be full of spelling errors. A fake invoice can look polished. A fake customer complaint can sound emotionally convincing. A fake job applicant can write beautifully. A fake vendor email can match the tone of a real business conversation. A fake executive request can sound urgent, reasonable, and familiar.

That changes the old warning signs.

For years, people were told to look for obvious mistakes. That advice is no longer enough. The new question is not only, "Does this look suspicious?" The new question is, "Has this been verified through the right channel?"

That difference is everything.

A modern business cannot rely on gut feeling alone. The message may sound right. The logo may look right. The writing may feel right. The pressure may feel real. But real security asks for proof, not just polish.

The owner does not need to do every technical task

This is where I want to relieve some pressure.

The business owner does not need to personally configure every setting, study every framework, monitor every log, or understand every attack technique. That is not the point. Leadership is not the same as doing every technical task.

But leadership does require ownership of the standard.

The owner should know what kind of information the business collects. The owner should know who is allowed to access sensitive systems. The owner should know how new tools are approved. The owner should know what happens when an employee leaves. The owner should know how payments are verified. The owner should know where customer data lives. The owner should know who is responsible when something goes wrong.

Those are not engineering questions. Those are governance questions.

When an owner refuses to own those questions, the business does not become simpler. It becomes dependent on luck, habits, and whoever happens to be paying attention that day.

The human-in-control principle

AI should make a business stronger, not less accountable.

That means the business has to decide where humans stay in control. Not because humans are perfect. We are not. But humans carry judgment, context, ethics, and responsibility in a way software cannot replace.

There are moments where automation is helpful. There are moments where automation should pause. There are moments where AI can draft, summarize, or recommend, but a person should approve. There are moments where the system should not be allowed to act until the right person has confirmed the truth.

That is not slowing the business down. That is protecting the business from moving fast in the wrong direction.

A healthy AI-powered business does not ask, "How much can we automate?" It asks, "Where should automation help, where should judgment remain, and how do we prove the difference?"

Security has to be built into operations

The old model treated security like a separate room.

Operations happened over here. Sales happened over there. Customer service happened somewhere else. Security was called when something broke, when a password stopped working, or when a suspicious email caused panic.

That model does not fit the AI era.

Security now has to live inside the daily rhythm of the business. It has to show up when tools are selected, when employees are onboarded, when access is granted, when customer information is collected, when automations are created, when files are shared, when payments are approved, when vendors are connected, and when AI systems are allowed to touch business data.

This is why the next generation of business systems cannot separate operations from protection. If a platform helps you move faster but cannot help you understand risk, it is only giving you half the picture.

The Aetis philosophy grows from that idea: the business should not have to choose between speed and security. The business needs an operating layer where visibility, action, accountability, and protection live together.

The cost of pretending it is too technical

One of the most dangerous sentences in business is, "I am not a tech person."

I say that gently because I know what people mean. The vocabulary can feel intimidating, and no owner wants to be made to feel behind.

But that sentence cannot become a permission slip to ignore the systems that run the company. You do not have to be a cybersecurity expert to lead responsibly, but you do need to know that access, data, verification, and accountability matter.

The owner who learns the language of responsibility becomes more trustworthy.

A practical definition of secure enough to grow

The goal is not to make a business impossible to attack. No honest security professional should promise that.

The goal is to make the business harder to misuse, easier to monitor, faster to recover, and clearer to govern.

That is what secure enough to grow really means.

It means people have the access they need and not much more. It means sensitive decisions require verification. It means data is not scattered everywhere without ownership. It means the business knows which tools matter. It means old access gets removed. It means AI systems are given boundaries. It means important activity is logged. It means the owner can ask a serious question and get a real answer instead of a shrug.

That is not paranoia. That is operational confidence.

The leadership shift

This chapter is not meant to turn every business owner into a security technician.

It is meant to make one thing clear: the owner can no longer treat cybersecurity as someone else's private technical island. If AI is part of the business, security is part of the business model. If data is part of the business, protection is part of the promise. If systems are making the business faster, governance has to make the business safer.

The leaders who understand this will have an advantage. They will not sound frantic. They will not sound paranoid. They will sound prepared.

And prepared is powerful.

The next threat

AI and cybersecurity are now connected to the daily life of the business owner.

But there is another layer underneath this conversation. It is one thing to use systems. It is another thing to depend on systems you do not understand.

That is where many modern businesses are standing right now. Their operations, money, customer relationships, marketing, scheduling, records, and decisions are increasingly shaped by tools they cannot fully explain, control, or verify.

In the next chapter, we will talk about what happens when your business depends on systems it does not understand, and why that dependency may become one of the defining leadership challenges of the AI era.

Part Three - The Threats

Chapter 15

When Your Business Depends on Systems It Does Not Understand

There is a moment that happens in a modern business that should make every owner pause.

Something goes wrong. A customer is charged twice. A message goes out with the wrong information. A team member loses access to a file they need. A report shows numbers that do not match what the owner expected. A lead disappears somewhere between the website, the inbox, and the customer system. Everyone begins asking the same question: why did that happen?

And then the room gets quiet.

Not because no one cares. Not because the team is lazy. Not because the business is badly run. The room gets quiet because nobody can fully explain the chain anymore. One person understands the payment tool. Another person understands the calendar. Someone else knows the marketing platform. A contractor set up the automations two years ago. The AI assistant is connected to a workflow, but nobody remembers exactly which one. The customer data lives in one place, the files live in another place, and the final decision somehow came from a system that everyone uses but no one can truly describe.

That is not science fiction. That is Tuesday for a lot of businesses now.

Understanding is now a leadership responsibility

For a long time, business owners could get away with not understanding every system inside the company. That was normal. The accountant understood the accounting software. The web person understood the website. The marketing person understood the email platform. The operations person understood the schedule. The owner understood the customers, the money, the people, and the direction.

That arrangement worked when systems stayed mostly in their own lanes.

AI changed that because systems no longer just store information. They talk to each other. They summarize. They recommend. They trigger. They route. They write. They flag. They score. They move faster than a person can manually supervise moment by moment.

That does not mean the owner has to become technical. I will say that again because it matters: the owner does not have to become technical. But the owner does have to become aware. There is a difference between not knowing how to code a system and not knowing what that system is allowed to do inside your business.

One is normal delegation. The other is blind dependency.

The black box problem

A black box is not always a bad tool. Many excellent systems are complex behind the scenes. You do not need to know every calculation your accounting software performs or every security rule your payment processor applies. Complexity itself is not the enemy.

The problem begins when the business cannot answer basic leadership questions about its own systems. What information does this tool use? Who can access it? What decisions does it influence? What happens when it is wrong? Who receives the alert? Who can override it? Where is the record kept? What happens if the vendor changes a rule, removes a feature, raises the price, or shuts down an integration?

Those are not programmer questions. Those are business questions.

When no one can answer them, the tool has quietly become more powerful than the process. That is the point where convenience turns into risk.

Convenience can become dependency

Most businesses do not become dependent all at once. Dependency usually arrives dressed as relief.

The owner is tired, so a tool that saves time feels like mercy. The team is overloaded, so an automation that removes repetitive work feels like progress. The inbox is chaos, so an AI summary feels like fresh air. The customer journey is messy, so a platform that promises to connect everything feels like a rescue boat.

And at first, it may be exactly that.

But the question is not whether a system helps. The question is whether the business still understands how the help is happening.

If a tool books appointments, the business should know what rules it follows. If a tool sends reminders, the business should know what triggers the message. If a tool scores leads, the business should know what behavior affects the score. If a tool drafts customer replies, the business should know what information it is allowed to use. If a tool blocks a transaction, the business should know who reviews the block and how the customer is treated while the issue is being reviewed.

Otherwise, the business is not operating with assistance. It is operating on assumption.

Borrowed logic still becomes your responsibility

This is one of the most important ideas in the AI era: when your business uses someone else's system, your customer still experiences it as your business.

The customer does not care that the scheduling tool glitched. They care that their appointment disappeared. The employee does not care that the access tool had a sync issue. They care that they cannot do their job. The client does not care that the automation pulled old data. They care that the proposal is wrong. The buyer does not care that an algorithm flagged them unfairly. They care that they were treated like a problem.

A vendor may build the tool, but the trust damage lands on the business using it.

That is why leadership cannot stop at asking, "Does this tool work?" Leaders have to ask, "What happens when this tool fails, misunderstands, or overreaches?"

That is where mature businesses separate themselves from careless businesses. They do not pretend systems will be perfect. They design around the reality that systems will sometimes be incomplete, outdated, biased, misconfigured, disconnected, or simply misunderstood by the humans using them.

When nobody knows why the system said no

One of the most dangerous phrases in modern business is, "The system will not let me."

Sometimes that phrase protects the business. A system should not let an unauthorized person see private records. It should not let a payment go through if something is obviously wrong. It should not let a team member bypass an approval step when money, privacy, or legal responsibility is involved.

But sometimes that phrase becomes a wall.

A customer is told no, but no one can explain the reason. An employee cannot complete a task, but no one knows what permission changed. A report blocks a decision, but no one knows whether the data is current. An AI-generated recommendation sounds confident, but no one knows what information shaped it.

That is not control. That is surrender with a dashboard.

A business does not need to override every system. That would defeat the purpose of having systems. But it does need an explanation path. It needs a way to understand what happened, why it happened, who is responsible for review, and what can be done when the system is wrong.

Integrations multiply responsibility

The modern business is not usually running on one system. It is running on a chain.

A customer fills out a form. That form sends information to a customer platform. The customer platform triggers an email. The email platform updates a score. The score changes a task. The task appears in a project board. The project board notifies a team member. The team member uploads a file. The file is summarized by AI. The summary informs a decision. The decision creates a record somewhere else.

That chain may feel smooth when everything works. But if something breaks, the business has to know where to look.

This is why fragmented tools are so expensive. The cost is not only subscription fees. The cost is confusion. The cost is time lost tracing a problem across five platforms. The cost is customer trust. The cost is staff frustration. The cost is decisions made from partial information because the full picture is hiding across a dozen screens.

In the AI era, integration without governance is not sophistication. It is exposure.

The employee who knows the system

There is another quiet dependency that businesses often overlook: the one person who knows how everything works.

Sometimes it is an employee. Sometimes it is a contractor. Sometimes it is the founder. Sometimes it is the assistant who has been holding the whole operation together with calendar links, spreadsheets, reminders, and private notes that nobody else understands.

That person is valuable, but the business cannot allow critical knowledge to live only in one mind.

If one person is the only map, the business is fragile. If one person is the only one who knows which tool sends which message, which automation touches which customer, which folder holds which contract, and which login controls which account, the business is not organized. It is personally dependent.

AI can make that problem worse if the business uses it to move faster without documenting the process. Suddenly the one person who knows the system is no longer only managing tools. They are managing tools that are managing other tools. That is too much invisible authority for any healthy business to leave undocumented.

Vendor promises are not governance

A polished software website can make any tool sound safe. It will promise simplicity, intelligence, automation, productivity, and security. Some of those promises may be true. But a vendor promise is not the same thing as business governance.

The vendor is responsible for its platform. The business is responsible for how that platform is used inside its operation.

That means the business still needs rules. It needs access boundaries. It needs review points. It needs records. It needs backup plans. It needs someone accountable for checking whether the tool is still serving the business instead of quietly reshaping the business around the tool.

This is especially important with AI because AI tools can feel more capable than they are. They can write beautifully and still miss the point. They can summarize quickly and leave out context. They can sound certain and still be wrong. They can help a business move faster, but speed is not the same thing as judgment.

A business that forgets that will eventually confuse automation with leadership.

The business needs an explanation layer

This is one reason I believe so strongly in the idea of a business control layer. Not because every company needs more software. Most companies already have too much software. What they need is a way to see the business clearly.

They need to know what systems exist, what each system does, who owns it, what data it touches, what decisions it influences, and what happens when something goes wrong. They need a practical map of the operation, not a technical encyclopedia that nobody reads.

An explanation layer gives the business language for its own machinery. It turns invisible workflows into visible responsibility. It helps leaders ask better questions before there is a crisis. It helps employees understand where their work fits. It helps customers feel the difference between a company that is guessing and a company that is governed.

This is part of the thinking behind Aetis: not simply protecting technology, but helping business owners operate with clarity, control, and trust in a world where the tools are moving faster than the old management habits were built to handle.

Control does not mean doing everything manually

Some people hear this conversation and think the answer is to stop using advanced tools. That is not the answer.

The answer is not to reject AI. The answer is not to go back to paper folders, manual reminders, and the old exhausted way of trying to remember everything. Businesses need better systems. Owners need leverage. Teams need relief. Customers expect speed. The future will not reward companies that refuse to modernize.

But it also will not reward companies that modernize without understanding what they have built.

Control means the business knows what is happening. It means the right people have authority and the wrong people do not. It means important decisions have human review. It means systems are documented well enough that the company is not held hostage by one vendor, one employee, one forgotten password, or one automation nobody remembers creating.

Control is not slowness. Control is confidence.

The leadership question

The question for the AI-era business owner is not, "Can I understand every technical detail?" That is the wrong question, and it will make smart people feel overwhelmed before they even begin.

The better question is, "Can my business explain the systems it depends on well enough to lead them responsibly?"

That is a different standard. It is practical. It is achievable. It does not require the owner to become a software engineer. It requires the owner to insist that the business be able to explain its own operation.

A business should know where its customer information lives. It should know who can change payment settings. It should know which automations touch customers. It should know what AI tools are allowed to see. It should know what happens when the system is wrong. It should know who can pause, review, correct, and document the issue.

That kind of clarity is not overkill. It is the new minimum for trustworthy growth.

The shift into human-in-control

The invisible war in business is not only about competitors, hackers, technology, or speed. It is also about whether the business can remain human-led while everything around it becomes more automated.

A company that depends on systems it does not understand will always be one problem away from panic. A company that understands its systems does not have to panic. It can investigate. It can explain. It can correct. It can improve. It can lead.

That is the real goal. Not fear. Not control for control's sake. Not technology worship. Leadership.

AI should make a business stronger, not stranger to itself.

So the next step is not simply to buy better tools. The next step is to build a business model where humans remain in command, judgment remains visible, and technology operates inside boundaries the business actually understands.

That is where we go next: the human-in-control business model.

Part Four - The Survival Framework

Chapter 16
The Human-in-Control Business Model

AI is most dangerous when people treat it like a replacement for leadership. It is most powerful when people treat it like an extension of leadership.

That distinction sounds simple until the pressure is real.

When the inbox is full, the calendar is packed, the customer is impatient, the team is waiting, the numbers are moving, and the software is offering a faster answer, it is tempting to let the machine take over more than it should. Not because the owner is careless. Not because the team is lazy. Because speed has a way of making surrender look efficient.

That is one of the biggest leadership tests of the AI era.

The businesses that survive this invisible war will not be the ones that reject AI. They will not be the ones that blindly hand everything to AI either. They will be the businesses that learn how to stay human at the center while allowing machines to carry the weight around them.

That is the heart of the human-in-control business model.

Control does not mean doing everything yourself

Many business owners hear the word control and immediately feel tired. They picture micromanaging every task, approving every message, watching every dashboard, and becoming the bottleneck they were trying to escape.

That is not control. That is exhaustion wearing a nice outfit.

Real control is not about touching every task. It is about knowing which decisions require human judgment, which decisions can be supported by AI, and which tasks can be automated without risking the soul of the business.

A human-in-control business does not make the owner the center of every click. It makes human judgment the center of the system.

That means the business has clear rules about what the machine can do alone, what it can recommend, what it can prepare, and what it must never decide without a person. It means automation serves the mission instead of quietly rewriting it. It means the company can move faster without becoming careless.

The goal is not to slow AI down. The goal is to give speed a steering wheel.

The owner is still the moral center

Every business has a moral center, even if the owner has never used those words. It shows up in how the company treats customers when something goes wrong. It shows up in whether the team is protected or exploited. It shows up in how refunds are handled, how promises are made, how privacy is respected, and how pressure is managed when money is tight.

AI does not naturally understand that center. It can learn patterns. It can imitate tone. It can summarize policies. It can produce language that sounds caring, professional, confident, or urgent. But it does not carry the responsibility of the business. The owner does.

That is why the human-in-control model begins with something deeper than software. It begins with the question, what kind of business are we building?

If the answer is unclear, AI will not fix it. AI will amplify the confusion. A business that does not know how it wants to serve customers will automate inconsistent service. A business that does not know what it values will automate whichever decision is fastest, cheapest, or easiest to measure. A business that does not know its boundaries will let every new tool push those boundaries a little farther.

The owner cannot outsource the soul of the company. They can use AI to express it, protect it, scale it, and support it. But they cannot ask AI to become it.

Judgment is the line in the sand

The simplest way to understand this model is to separate labor from judgment.

Labor is the work that can be described, repeated, organized, summarized, routed, drafted, compared, checked, scheduled, or monitored. AI is very good at helping with labor, especially labor that drains attention without requiring wisdom.

Judgment is different. Judgment decides what matters. Judgment weighs context. Judgment understands consequences. Judgment knows when the technically correct answer is still the wrong answer for this customer, this employee, this moment, or this relationship.

A machine can help prepare a response to an upset client. A human should decide whether that response honors the relationship. A machine can flag a suspicious transaction. A human should decide how aggressively to act when a long-time customer may be involved. A machine can recommend a cost reduction. A human should decide whether the savings are worth the damage to quality, morale, or trust.

That is not anti-AI. That is mature AI.

The companies that will get hurt are not always the ones with weak tools. They are the ones with weak lines. They never decide where the machine stops and the person begins. So the line moves on its own. First AI drafts. Then AI sends. Then AI decides. Then AI explains what happened after the damage is already done.

A human-in-control business draws the line before the pressure hits.

The approval layer becomes a business asset

In the old business world, approvals were often treated like friction. A manager had to sign off. An owner had to review. A department had to confirm. Everyone wanted fewer approvals because approvals slowed things down.

In the AI era, approvals become something more valuable. They become the trust layer.

That does not mean every tiny action needs a meeting. It means the business designs approvals around risk. Low-risk work can move quickly. Medium-risk work can be reviewed. High-risk work must be approved by someone accountable. The point is not to create red tape. The point is to make sure the business does not accidentally automate decisions that carry legal, financial, reputational, or human consequences.

A customer email may not need approval if it confirms a shipping update. It may need review if it discusses a refund dispute. It should need human approval if it admits fault, threatens action, changes contract terms, or handles sensitive information.

An employee workflow may not need approval if it schedules routine training. It may need review if it changes access permissions. It should need human approval if it affects pay, discipline, hiring, firing, or personal data.

This is where many businesses will either mature or stumble. They will either build approval into their operating rhythm, or they will wait until a machine-speed mistake forces them to explain why no one was watching.

The human-in-control business has memory

Control also requires memory. A business cannot stay in control if it cannot see what happened, who approved it, what changed, and why the decision was made.

This is where AI can be incredibly useful when it is designed correctly. It can help create a living memory of the business. It can summarize conversations, track decisions, preserve context, and connect activity across departments. But that memory must be organized and protected. Otherwise it becomes another pile of digital clutter.

A business with memory can answer basic questions without panic. What did we promise this client? Who changed the workflow? Why did the system send that message? When did the policy update? What data was used? Who approved the exception?

Those questions matter because trust often breaks after the fact. A customer rarely asks for your internal process when everything goes well. They ask when something goes wrong. A regulator, insurer, partner, investor, or attorney asks when the stakes are already higher. A team member asks when a decision feels unfair or confusing.

The business that can answer clearly has an advantage. Not because it is perfect, but because it is accountable.

That is one reason I care so much about systems that protect the record of the business. Not just the flashy front end. Not just the dashboard. The record. The memory. The audit trail. The proof that decisions were made with intention rather than chaos.

AI should make people more capable, not less responsible

There is a lazy version of AI adoption that says, use the machine so people do not have to think. That version may look efficient for a little while, but it weakens the business over time.

The stronger version says, use the machine so people can think better.

That is a very different model. In the stronger model, AI handles preparation, comparison, drafting, reminders, summaries, checks, and routine coordination. The person still brings context, care, ethics, taste, business sense, and responsibility. The machine reduces the noise so the human can make a better decision.

A good AI system should make a customer service representative more prepared, not more robotic. It should make a manager more aware, not more detached. It should make an owner more informed, not more absent. It should make the business faster without making it colder.

This matters because customers can feel when a company has automated the person out of the relationship. They may not know which system is being used. They may not know what workflow is running behind the scenes. But they can feel when no one is actually listening.

Human-in-control does not mean every interaction is hand-written from scratch. It means every interaction is still governed by human standards.

The framework starts with deciding what must remain human

Before a business buys another AI tool, it should pause and decide what must remain human.

That question is more powerful than it looks. It forces the owner to identify the parts of the business that carry trust. It brings the invisible work into the open. It helps the team understand where speed is welcome and where care matters more than speed.

For some businesses, the human center may be customer complaints, refunds, pricing exceptions, hiring decisions, security access, financial approvals, medical or legal communications, or anything involving sensitive personal information. For another business, it may be creative direction, brand voice, client relationships, negotiation, or strategic partnerships.

There is no universal answer because every business has a different trust promise. But every business needs an answer.

Once that answer exists, AI adoption becomes much cleaner. The business is no longer asking, what can this tool do? It is asking, where does this tool fit inside the kind of company we are building?

That shift changes everything. The owner stops chasing features and starts designing an operating model.

The owner does not need to become a technician

I want to be very clear about something because this is where many people start to feel overwhelmed. A human-in-control business does not require the owner to become a software engineer.

The owner does not need to know every model architecture, every integration method, every security protocol, or every technical term. That is not the job. The job is to understand enough to lead the system responsibly.

A restaurant owner does not have to manufacture the oven to know whether the kitchen is safe. A trucking company owner does not have to build the engine to know maintenance matters. A business owner does not have to write every line of code to know whether AI is handling customer data, changing decisions, or creating risk.

The leadership questions are plain English. What is this tool allowed to do? What information does it use? Who checks the output? What happens when it is wrong? Where is the record kept? Who can override it? What decisions are off-limits?

Those questions do not make the owner technical. They make the owner awake.

And awake is the minimum standard now.

The calm business beats the frantic business

The human-in-control model also creates calm. That may sound soft, but calm is a competitive advantage in a machine-speed world.

A frantic business reacts to every notification, every new AI trend, every competitor announcement, and every vendor promise. It bolts tools onto broken processes. It automates work it has never properly understood. It confuses activity with progress.

A calm business moves differently. It knows what it is trying to protect. It knows which decisions matter. It knows where AI can help. It knows where humans must stay involved. It does not need to panic every time the market changes because its foundation is not built on hype. It is built on clarity.

That kind of calm does not happen by accident. It comes from designing the business brain, the approvals, the memory, the roles, the workflows, and the security around the way the company actually operates.

This is where the invisible war becomes very practical. The fight is not only between companies with AI and companies without AI. It is between companies that have an operating model and companies that have a pile of tools.

The pile of tools may look impressive. The operating model wins.

The next move is building the business brain

Once the owner accepts that human judgment must stay at the center, the next question is obvious. How does the business organize its knowledge so AI can support the right things without creating more chaos?

That is where the business brain comes in.

A business brain is not a cute phrase for a folder full of documents. It is the organized intelligence of the company. It is where policies, processes, customer knowledge, team responsibilities, financial rules, security standards, brand voice, approvals, and operating memory begin to work together instead of living in disconnected places.

Without a business brain, AI is guessing from fragments. With a business brain, AI has context. Without a business brain, automation magnifies confusion. With a business brain, automation can support clarity. Without a business brain, the owner keeps explaining the same things over and over. With a business brain, the business begins to remember.

That is the next step in the survival framework. Not more noise. Not more apps. Not another shiny promise.

A business that wants to move at machine speed without losing its humanity must first build the place where its knowledge, judgment, and standards live.

That is what we will build next.

Part Four - The Survival Framework

Chapter 17

Build the Business Brain

A business cannot move at machine speed if its memory is scattered across inboxes, sticky notes, chat threads, file folders, people's heads, and six different apps that barely speak to each other.

That is not a technology problem first. It is an operating problem.

Most business owners do not realize how much of their company lives in fragments until they try to use AI in a serious way. At first, AI feels powerful because it can write, summarize, organize, draft, explain, and suggest. Then the owner asks it to help with something important, and the real question appears underneath the request. Where is the truth of this business?

Where is the current pricing? Where is the actual refund policy? Where is the latest version of the service agreement? Where are the customer notes that matter? Where are the security rules? Where are the employee responsibilities? Where is the difference between what the company says publicly and what it does privately?

If the answer is, "Let me check three places and ask two people," then AI is not the issue. The business brain has not been built yet.

A business brain is the organized intelligence of the company. It is not a cute name for cloud storage. It is not a folder labeled important. It is not a pile of documents that everyone swears they will clean up later. A business brain is the living structure that tells the company what it knows, how it operates, what it protects, who is allowed to decide, and how work should move.

When that brain exists, AI becomes dramatically more useful. When it does not exist, AI becomes a very fast assistant trapped inside a messy office.

Your business already has a brain

Every business already has a brain. The question is whether that brain is designed or accidental.

In many small businesses, the brain is the owner. The owner remembers which customer needs special handling. The owner knows which vendor is reliable. The owner knows why one product is priced differently from another. The owner knows which employee can handle pressure, which client needs extra reassurance, and which decision should never be made without a second look.

That works for a while because the owner is close to everything. It may even feel like an advantage. Customers like that the owner remembers them. Employees like that the owner can answer quickly. The business feels personal, responsive, and alive.

But there is a hidden limit inside that model. If the business brain lives mostly inside one person, the business can only scale as far as that person's attention can stretch.

That is where good businesses begin to feel strangely heavy. The owner is not failing. The owner is carrying memory, judgment, coordination, history, quality control, customer care, vendor knowledge, financial awareness, and risk management all at the same time. Even before AI enters the picture, that is too much for one human nervous system to hold.

AI does not remove that burden automatically. In fact, AI can make it more obvious. A tool can draft the email, but it does not know the customer history unless the business knows where that history lives. A tool can summarize a process, but it cannot protect the process if five versions exist. A tool can recommend a decision, but it cannot honor the company's values if those values are not written into the way the company operates.

Building the business brain means taking what has been trapped in memory, habit, and scattered systems and turning it into a structure the company can actually use.

The business brain is not just information

This is where many people make the first mistake. They think building a business brain means collecting information. So they start uploading files, saving notes, making folders, and dumping documents into a platform. That may feel productive, but a pile of information is not a brain.

A brain does not merely store facts. A brain connects meaning. It understands relationships. It knows what matters now and what is old. It knows which signal deserves attention and which noise can be ignored. It knows when something is normal and when something is off.

Your business brain has to do the same thing.

It should not only know that you have a customer service policy. It should know which version is current, who can change it, when it applies, what exceptions require approval, and how that policy connects to refunds, reputation, cash flow, and trust. It should not only know that your company uses certain tools. It should know who has access, what data those tools touch, what happens when someone leaves, and which workflows depend on them.

This is why AI strategy cannot be separated from operational design. If the company does not know how its own knowledge is organized, AI will not magically organize it. AI may create the appearance of order. It may produce a clean summary. It may make a beautiful chart. But underneath, the business may still be operating from confusion.

A business brain gives AI something better to work with than fragments. It gives AI context.

Context is what turns a generic answer into a useful answer. Context is what keeps automation from treating every customer the same. Context is what helps a system understand that two tasks may look similar on the surface but carry very different consequences. Context is the difference between software that responds and software that serves.

Start with the decisions that repeat

The easiest way to begin is not by trying to document the entire company at once. That will overwhelm almost anyone. The better starting point is to look for the decisions that repeat.

Every business has them. The same customer questions. The same approval points. The same pricing confusion. The same intake process. The same follow-up sequence. The same handoff between people. The same monthly financial review. The same hiring steps. The same security checks that everyone agrees are important but nobody wants to chase.

These repeated decisions are where the business brain begins to form.

When a decision repeats, it deserves a home. It should not live as a vague memory or a buried message. It should be clear enough that a person can follow it, an AI system can support it, and the owner can audit it later. That does not mean turning the business into a cold machine. It means giving the company a way to remember what good judgment looks like when the day gets busy.

For example, if your team handles customer complaints, the business brain should not simply say, "be nice to customers." That is not enough. It should capture how the company listens, what tone it uses, when it apologizes, what it can offer, when a refund is appropriate, when an issue must be escalated, and what should never be promised just to make a problem go away.

That kind of clarity protects everyone. It protects the customer from being treated differently depending on who answers. It protects the employee from guessing under pressure. It protects the owner from becoming the emergency answer machine. It protects the brand from inconsistency. And when AI is used, it gives the system guardrails that are rooted in the actual business, not in generic best practices.

The brain needs memory and boundaries

A strong business brain has two sides. It has memory, and it has boundaries.

Memory is what the business knows. It includes the company story, offers, customers, policies, workflows, contracts, financial rules, standards, lessons learned, and decisions that should not have to be rediscovered every month. Memory makes the business less dependent on constant explanation. It lets new team members come up to speed faster. It helps AI provide support that sounds like the company instead of sounding like the internet.

Boundaries are what the business refuses to risk. They include privacy rules, approval limits, access controls, brand standards, legal obligations, security requirements, and ethical lines. Boundaries tell AI and people where speed must stop and judgment must step in.

Many companies build memory without boundaries. They collect information, connect tools, and automate tasks, but they do not define what should be protected. That creates exposure. Other companies build boundaries without memory. They have rules, restrictions, and warnings, but the business still cannot move because nobody can find what they need. That creates friction.

The goal is both. Memory without boundaries is risky. Boundaries without memory are slow. A business brain needs to know what the company knows and what the company will not compromise.

This matters because AI will always be pulled toward completion. Give it a task, and it tries to finish. That is useful when the task is low-risk. It is dangerous when the task touches money, privacy, reputation, contracts, employment, or customer trust. The business brain must tell the system when completion is not the highest value. Sometimes the highest value is accuracy. Sometimes it is approval. Sometimes it is restraint. Sometimes it is saying, "A person needs to review this."

The owner does not have to become the database

One fear I see in business owners is the fear that organizing the business brain will create more work. They imagine endless documentation, complicated dashboards, and a second job maintaining the system that was supposed to make life easier.

That fear is reasonable. Plenty of businesses have been buried by systems that were too elaborate for the way they actually worked. A useful business brain should not make the owner feel like they are serving the software. The software should serve the business.

The practical starting point is simple: capture what is already being repeated.

If you answer the same customer question every week, that belongs in the business brain. If you explain the same process to every new hire, that belongs there. If you keep checking the same spreadsheet before making the same decision, that belongs there. If a mistake keeps happening because people do not know the rule, that rule belongs there. If the owner keeps saying, "I thought everyone knew that," it probably belongs there too.

The business brain is not built by locking yourself in a room and writing a perfect manual. It is built by paying attention to the places where the company keeps repeating itself, confusing itself, or depending on one person to remember everything.

That is also why the process should feel alive. A business brain is never finished in the same way a business is never finished. It should evolve as the company grows, learns, launches new offers, hires new people, changes tools, enters new markets, and faces new risks. The point is not perfection. The point is a reliable place for truth to live.

AI should plug into the brain, not replace it

Once the business brain begins to exist, AI can finally become more than a novelty.

It can help draft based on the company's real voice. It can help onboard employees using current processes. It can help summarize customer history before a call. It can help spot gaps in workflows. It can help prepare decisions for human review. It can help compare what was promised against what was delivered. It can help surface risk before the owner has to discover it the hard way.

But notice the direction. AI plugs into the brain. It does not become the brain.

That distinction matters. If AI becomes the brain, the company slowly loses its own understanding. People stop knowing why decisions are made. Policies become whatever the tool says. Workflows become whatever the automation allows. The business may move faster, but it becomes dependent in a way that is hard to see until something breaks.

When AI plugs into the business brain, the company stays in charge. The owner and team define the truth, the standards, the approvals, and the boundaries. AI helps carry, organize, and activate that intelligence. The machine supports the operating model instead of quietly becoming the operating model.

This is one of the reasons I believe the future belongs to businesses that treat AI as infrastructure, not entertainment. The winners will not simply be the companies with the flashiest prompts. They will be the companies that know how to connect their knowledge, protect their trust, and give their teams a clear place to think from.

A business that remembers can grow

Growth exposes memory problems. A small team can survive on informal knowledge for a while. A growing team cannot. More customers create more exceptions. More employees create more handoffs. More tools create more access points. More revenue creates more responsibility. More speed creates more opportunity for small mistakes to become expensive.

A business that remembers can absorb growth with more stability. It can train better. It can serve more consistently. It can delegate without losing control. It can automate without becoming reckless. It can protect customers because it knows what it promised them. It can protect employees because expectations are not hidden in the owner's head. It can protect the owner because leadership is no longer confused with remembering every detail alone.

This is where AI and business maturity meet.

A mature business does not use AI to cover up chaos. It uses AI to activate clarity. It does not ask the machine to invent the company every morning. It gives the machine a responsible structure to work within. It does not confuse speed with intelligence. It builds intelligence first, then lets speed serve it.

That is the real promise of the business brain. It gives the company a center. It gives the team a shared memory. It gives AI the context it needs. It gives the owner room to lead instead of constantly translating the business to everyone and everything around them.

In the AI era, the businesses that win will not be the ones with the most scattered tools. They will be the ones with the clearest operating intelligence.

Build the brain, and the business can finally stop starting over every day.

Build the brain, and AI becomes useful in a way that is grounded, safe, and scalable.

Build the brain, and the company begins to do something every strong organization must eventually learn how to do.

It begins to remember.

Part Four - The Survival Framework

Chapter 18

Automate the Repetitive. Protect the Judgment.

Automation sounds glamorous until you see what happens when a business automates the wrong thing.

At first, it feels like magic. The software answers faster. The message goes out on time. The invoice gets created without anyone touching it. The reminder appears before the client has to ask. The report that used to eat half a morning shows up in minutes. For a tired business owner, that can feel like oxygen.

And it is powerful. I do not want to minimize that. Repetition drains people. It eats the best hours of the day and gives back very little pride. Most owners did not start their company because they loved copying information from one place to another, chasing signatures, reminding people about the same deadlines, or digging through email threads for the fifth version of a document. They started because they had judgment, skill, a service, a product, a mission, a gift, or a problem they knew how to solve.

So when AI and automation step in and say, I can take some of that off your plate, the answer should not automatically be fear. Sometimes the answer should be, thank you, where have you been?

But there is a difference between taking work off your plate and taking responsibility out of your hands. That difference is where many businesses will either become stronger or quietly become dangerous.

The future does not belong to the business that automates the most. It belongs to the business that knows what should be automated and what should remain protected by human judgment.

Automation is not the goal

One of the biggest mistakes business owners make with new technology is turning the tool into the mission. A new platform appears, a new app gets recommended, a new AI feature launches, and suddenly the conversation becomes, How much can we automate?

That is the wrong first question.

The better question is, What kind of business are we trying to become?

If the goal is to become faster at serving customers, automation can help. If the goal is to reduce dropped balls, automation can help. If the goal is to give the owner back enough mental space to lead again, automation can help. If the goal is to create a more consistent experience, automation can help. But if the goal is simply to remove people from the process because people are expensive or inconvenient, the business is already moving in the wrong direction.

Automation is not leadership. Automation is not wisdom. Automation is not culture. Automation is not trust. Automation is a way to move defined work through a defined system with less friction.

That sentence matters because the word defined is doing a lot of work.

If a task is not understood, automating it does not make it better. If a process is messy, automation can make the mess travel faster. If the data is wrong, automation can spread the error with confidence. If the responsibility is unclear, automation can make everyone feel like nobody is responsible.

This is why I do not believe business owners should start by asking, What can AI do for me? They should start by asking, What do we already repeat, what do we already understand, and where are we wasting human attention?

Repetition is where AI earns its keep

There is a category of work that is important but not deeply human. It needs to happen. It needs to be accurate. It needs to be timely. But it does not need a person's full creativity, empathy, or judgment every single time.

Appointment reminders fall into that category. Status updates often fall into that category. First drafts of routine messages can fall into that category. Data cleanup, document sorting, task routing, calendar coordination, receipt organization, basic reporting, lead intake, follow-up prompts, internal reminders, and recurring checklists can all fall into that category when the rules are clear.

This is where automation becomes a gift. It gives back the hours that were being spent on work people could do, but should not have to do manually forever.

A good automation removes drag. It does not remove care.

That is a key distinction. When a client receives an automatic reminder, the client should feel supported, not processed. When an employee receives an automatic task, the employee should feel clear, not controlled. When the owner receives an automated dashboard, the owner should feel informed, not replaced by numbers.

The best automation is almost invisible. It does not call attention to itself. It simply keeps the business from depending on memory, panic, and last-minute heroics.

That is the part I want everyday business owners to understand. You do not need automation so you can become cold or robotic. You need automation so your humanity is not trapped under the weight of things a system could have handled for you.

Judgment is where the human stays

Now we need to talk about the work that should not be casually handed over.

Judgment lives in the moments where the rules are not enough. It lives in the exception. It lives in the uncomfortable customer complaint. It lives in the employee who is technically late but has a real family crisis. It lives in the refund request that meets the written policy but violates the spirit of the relationship. It lives in the security alert that might be harmless, or might be the first sign of something serious. It lives in the financial decision that affects payroll, reputation, trust, or someone's future.

AI can support those moments. It can summarize. It can surface context. It can show the policy. It can compare options. It can remind you what happened last time. It can help you think.

But it should not become the conscience of the business.

That line may sound dramatic, but it is not. Every business has a conscience, whether the owner has named it or not. It shows up in how the business treats people when things go wrong. It shows up in what the company is willing to do for money and what it refuses to do even when there is pressure. It shows up in whether the customer is treated like a transaction or a relationship.

If you automate judgment too aggressively, the business can begin making decisions that are technically efficient but emotionally careless. Customers feel it. Employees feel it. Partners feel it. And once trust is damaged, the fact that the workflow was efficient does not matter very much.

Protecting judgment means deciding, in advance, where a human must remain accountable. It means certain decisions require review. Certain messages require approval. Certain exceptions require a person. Certain risks require escalation. Certain customer moments require a voice, not just a response.

The owner cannot approve everything

There is an important balance here because the answer cannot be, The owner must personally approve every automated action.

That is not a system. That is a bottleneck wearing a responsible outfit.

A business cannot scale if every question, every exception, every message, and every decision has to climb back to one person. That is how owners become trapped inside the very company they built. They are technically in charge, but practically buried. Their phone becomes the control room. Their inbox becomes the operating system. Their memory becomes the database. Their anxiety becomes the alert system.

The answer is not to keep everything manual. The answer is to design levels of authority.

Some automations should run freely because the risk is low and the rules are clear. Some should run but leave a visible record. Some should prepare the work but wait for approval. Some should alert a manager when the conditions change. Some should stop entirely and require a human decision.

That is how a mature business thinks. Not everything is treated the same. A welcome email is not a contract change. A reminder is not a termination notice. A draft is not a final decision. A recommendation is not an order. A pattern is not proof.

When a business understands those differences, automation becomes disciplined. It becomes a system of support instead of a system of blind motion.

Do not automate what you have not cleaned up

This is where Chapter 17 becomes practical. Before you automate, you need the business brain to know what is true.

If your refund policy exists in three different places, which one should AI follow? If your sales team uses one version of the offer and operations uses another, which version should automation send to the customer? If your customer records are incomplete, who should receive the follow-up? If your permissions are loose, who is allowed to trigger the workflow? If nobody owns the process, who fixes it when it breaks?

These questions are not glamorous, but they are the difference between a business that becomes more powerful with AI and a business that becomes more chaotic with AI.

Automation loves clarity. It struggles with contradiction. If your business has been surviving on informal knowledge, side conversations, and people just knowing what to do, AI will expose the weak spots. That exposure can feel uncomfortable, but it is also useful. It tells you where the business has been depending on memory instead of structure.

Do not treat that as an embarrassment. Treat it as a map.

Every place where the business says, We are not sure, is a place to define the process. Every place where the team says, Ask Sarah, because she knows, is a place to capture knowledge. Every place where customers get different answers is a place to create consistency. Every place where decisions happen without a record is a place to build accountability.

Once that is done, automation has something worth following.

Speed needs a brake

There is a reason cars have brakes. The brake is not the enemy of speed. The brake is what makes speed usable.

A business that wants to operate with AI needs the same mindset. The goal is not to go as fast as possible in every direction. The goal is to move quickly where speed helps and slow down where trust requires it.

A good AI-enabled business has brakes built into the system. It has approval gates. It has audit trails. It has permission levels. It has limits on who can change what. It has a way to see what happened. It has a way to pause a workflow when something looks wrong. It has a way for a human to override the machine when the machine does not understand the full story.

That is not overengineering. That is responsible design.

This is one of the reasons I care so deeply about building systems that combine business operations with security thinking. In the old world, people treated operations and cybersecurity as separate conversations. Operations was about getting work done. Cybersecurity was about keeping bad things out.

In the AI era, those conversations merge. The same automation that sends the right document faster could also send the wrong document to the wrong person if permissions are careless. The same AI that helps summarize a customer file could expose sensitive information if the data layer is sloppy. The same workflow that saves time could create risk if nobody can see who approved what.

The business of the future does not just ask, Can this be automated? It asks, Can this be automated safely, clearly, and accountably?

Automation should make people more present

The best use of automation is not to make a business feel less human. It is to give humans enough room to be human again.

When the repetitive work is handled, the owner can think. The manager can coach. The employee can serve. The team can notice patterns. The customer can receive attention before frustration builds. The business can stop operating as if everyone is one missed reminder away from a problem.

That is the emotional promise of good automation. It lowers the noise.

A business owner who is drowning in repetitive work often sounds short, distracted, and reactive, even when that is not who they are. A team buried in manual tasks can look careless, even when they care deeply. A company with no automation can appear disorganized, even when the people inside it are working hard.

Automation cannot fix a bad heart. But it can reduce the friction that keeps good people from showing up at their best.

That is why I want business owners to think of automation as protection for attention. Your attention is one of the most valuable resources in the company. Once it is scattered, everything suffers. Decisions get weaker. Communication gets thinner. Strategy gets delayed. The owner becomes reactive instead of intentional.

Use automation to protect the attention that should be spent on judgment, relationships, strategy, and trust.

The chapter in one sentence

If you remember nothing else from this chapter, remember this: automate the repeatable work so humans can protect the meaningful work.

That is the model. Not humans versus machines. Not owners versus tools. Not speed versus care. The right model is disciplined partnership.

Let AI help the business move. Let automation carry the routine. Let systems remember what people should not have to keep in their heads. Let software prepare the draft, surface the context, route the task, catch the deadline, and organize the signal.

But keep humans responsible for the moments where trust is on the line.

The businesses that understand this will feel different. Customers will feel served, not processed. Employees will feel supported, not replaced. Owners will feel more in command, not less. And the company will move faster without becoming reckless.

That is the kind of business the AI era is asking us to build.

But to build it, automation cannot float on top of a weak foundation. It needs the right stack underneath it. It needs secure tools, clean data, permission control, visibility, and accountability. That is where we go next.

Part Four - The Survival Framework

Chapter 19
The Secure AI Stack

A secure AI stack is not a pile of software. It is the way a business decides what its technology is allowed to know, allowed to do, allowed to touch, and allowed to change.

That may sound simple, but it is one of the biggest dividing lines in the AI era. Some businesses will add AI the way people add another app to their phone. They will sign in, connect a few tools, paste in customer information, upload files, automate a workflow, and hope the convenience outweighs the risk. They will move quickly, and for a while, it may feel like progress.

Other businesses will pause long enough to ask a better question. Before we let this system move faster, what is it connected to?

That question changes everything. It turns AI from a shiny feature into an operating decision. It forces the owner to think about data, permissions, vendors, employees, customers, security, accountability, and recovery. It makes the business look underneath the excitement and ask whether the foundation is strong enough to carry the speed.

I want to make this very approachable because the phrase secure AI stack can sound like something only a large company with a technology department should care about. That is not true. Every business using AI has a stack, even if nobody has named it. A one-person company has a stack. A small shop has a stack. A growing service business has a stack. A real estate office, salon, nonprofit, law firm, clinic, construction company, coaching business, or online store has a stack.

The stack is simply the chain of tools, data, people, rules, and decisions that make the business run. In the old world, a weak stack made the business inefficient. In the AI era, a weak stack can make the business exposed.

Start with what the system can see

Before a business asks what AI can do, it should ask what AI can see.

That is where security begins. Not with fear. Not with panic. Not with a complicated dashboard full of language nobody understands. It begins with visibility. What data are we feeding into these tools? What files are being uploaded? What customer conversations are being summarized? What financial information is being connected? What employee information is inside the system? What private strategy, pricing, contracts, or internal decisions are being exposed to tools we do not fully control?

Many business owners do not think about this because the interface feels harmless. It looks like a chat box. It feels like asking a smart assistant for help. But behind that simple experience is a system receiving information. Sometimes that information is ordinary. Sometimes it is sensitive. Sometimes the owner knows exactly what is being shared. Sometimes the sharing happens casually because someone on the team is trying to save time.

This is how risk enters quietly. Not because someone is irresponsible, but because convenience moves faster than policy.

A secure AI stack begins by deciding what information can go where. Public information can be treated one way. Internal information needs more care. Customer data needs stronger protection. Financial data needs stronger protection. Employee data needs stronger protection. Legal, medical, identity, security, and proprietary information need the highest level of caution.

The owner does not need to become a cybersecurity engineer to understand that. The owner simply needs to respect the difference between information that can be shared broadly and information that must be handled like trust.

Permissions are business decisions

One of the most overlooked parts of an AI-enabled business is permission control.

Who is allowed to see customer records? Who can connect a tool to the company email? Who can export reports? Who can approve an automation? Who can change a workflow? Who can upload contracts? Who can invite another app into the business? Who can delete information? Who can override a system recommendation?

Those questions may sound administrative, but they are leadership questions. Permissions are not just technical settings. They are business decisions about trust, authority, and risk.

In a small business, permissions are often loose because everyone is busy and everyone is helping. That can work for a season, especially when the company is young. But once AI enters the environment, loose permissions become more dangerous. A person who can access everything may accidentally feed everything into the wrong place. A person who can connect apps may give a vendor more access than intended. A person who can approve an automation may create a workflow that sends information too broadly.

The goal is not to treat employees like threats. The goal is to stop forcing good people to operate inside risky systems.

A strong business does not give every person every key. It gives people the access they need to do their work well, then builds guardrails around the areas where mistakes would be expensive. That protects the company, but it also protects the team. Clear permissions reduce confusion, blame, and accidental exposure.

In the AI era, permission design is part of culture. It tells people, We trust you enough to give you the right tools, and we respect the business enough not to make access careless.

The vendor is part of the stack

Every tool you connect becomes part of the business environment.

That matters because a company can be careful internally and still create risk through the vendors it trusts. An AI writing tool, scheduling tool, customer service tool, bookkeeping tool, CRM, payroll platform, file storage platform, analytics platform, automation tool, or chatbot can all become part of the chain. If one part of the chain is weak, the business can feel it.

Most owners do not have time to read every technical document behind every vendor. I understand that. But they can still ask practical questions. Does this tool need access to sensitive data? Does it explain how data is handled? Can access be limited by role? Can the business export its information if it leaves? Can activity be reviewed? Can accounts be removed quickly when someone leaves the team? Does the tool support stronger login protection? Does it have a reputation for reliability?

Those are not fancy questions. They are common-sense questions. They help the owner avoid building the company on tools that feel easy today but become painful later.

The cheapest tool is not always the least expensive tool. A low-cost platform that creates confusion, exposes data, locks information away, or fails during an important moment can become very expensive very quickly.

This is why the secure AI stack is also a business stack. Security is not separate from operations. The tool that holds your customer data affects sales. The tool that holds your documents affects service. The tool that routes work affects delivery. The tool that connects to payments affects trust. Once a system touches the business, it is no longer just software. It is part of how the business keeps its promises.

Visibility is the control room

A business cannot protect what it cannot see.

That sentence is simple, but it should sit at the center of every AI strategy. If a business does not know what tools are being used, what data is being shared, what automations are running, what decisions are being recommended, or who has access to what, it is not operating with control. It is operating with hope.

Hope is not a strategy, especially when systems are moving at machine speed.

The secure AI stack needs visibility. Not surveillance in a creepy way. Not micromanagement. Visibility means the owner or leadership team can understand the operating environment. They can see the major tools. They can see the sensitive workflows. They can see approvals. They can see alerts. They can see when someone changes something important. They can see enough to ask good questions before a small issue becomes a large problem.

This is where audit trails matter. An audit trail is simply a record of what happened. Who changed the setting? Who approved the release? Who connected the tool? Who viewed the file? Who sent the message? Who changed the customer status? Who overrode the recommendation?

When everything goes well, records may feel boring. When something goes wrong, records become priceless.

They help a business respond calmly. They reduce guessing. They protect honest people. They show patterns. They make accountability possible without turning every problem into a blame game.

A secure AI stack does not depend on memory. It creates a visible path.

Security should feel like structure, not fear

One reason business owners avoid security conversations is that security is often presented in a way that feels intimidating. It sounds expensive, technical, and judgmental. The owner hears a language of threats, acronyms, frameworks, and worst-case scenarios, then quietly decides to deal with it later.

I understand that reaction. But in this book, I want to frame security differently.

Security is structure. It is how the business protects trust while it grows. It is how the company makes sure people have the right access, information goes to the right place, customers are respected, employees are protected, vendors are chosen carefully, and mistakes can be caught before they become disasters.

That is not fear. That is maturity.

A secure AI stack does not need to make the business slow. In fact, it can do the opposite. When roles are clear, people move faster. When data is organized, AI becomes more useful. When approvals are built in, decisions do not get stuck in panic. When tools are chosen well, the team is not constantly patching around broken systems. When access is controlled, the owner does not have to rely on luck.

Good security creates confidence. It allows the business to say yes to speed because the brakes, mirrors, and seatbelts are already in place.

The simple architecture of trust

If you strip away the technical language, the secure AI stack is built on a simple architecture of trust.

First, the business knows what information matters. Second, it decides where that information is allowed to go. Third, it gives people the right level of access. Fourth, it chooses tools that can be trusted with the role they are being given. Fifth, it keeps records of important activity. Sixth, it has a way to pause, recover, and correct when something goes wrong.

That is not a list to memorize. It is a way of thinking.

The business owner should be able to look at any AI tool and ask, Where does this sit in our trust architecture? Is it touching public information, internal information, customer information, financial information, employee information, or strategic information? Is it helping us draft, decide, route, approve, store, analyze, or act? Who is responsible for it? What happens if it makes a mistake? What happens if we stop using it?

Those questions turn AI from a toy into infrastructure.

That is the shift mature businesses will make. They will stop treating AI as something floating above the business and start treating it as something embedded inside the business. Once it is embedded, it must be governed.

Governance does not have to mean bureaucracy. It means grown-up ownership. It means the business is not sleepwalking into dependence. It means someone understands the role of the system, the risk of the system, and the value of the system.

Aetis and the reason this matters

This is one of the reasons I see AI, cybersecurity, and business operations as one conversation.

When I think about the future of business, I do not see a world where owners can afford to keep everything separate. One tool for operations. Another tool for security. Another tool for data. Another tool for compliance. Another tool for workflow. Another tool for visibility. Another tool for customer communication. Another tool for financial organization. Every separate piece creates another gap the owner has to understand, manage, and protect.

That is part of what shaped the way I think about systems like Aetis. The point is not to make business more complicated. The point is to create a clearer control layer for the modern company, where protection, operations, workflow, data, and accountability are not fighting each other. They are working together.

A business owner should not have to become a full-time systems detective just to understand how the company is running. The future should make owners more informed, not more overwhelmed.

That does not mean every business needs the same platform, the same budget, or the same level of sophistication. A small company and a large enterprise will build differently. But the principle is the same. The business needs a secure foundation before it trusts AI with more work.

Without that foundation, AI becomes another layer of noise. With that foundation, AI becomes leverage.

Do not wait until the business is big

Many owners make the mistake of thinking they will get serious about structure later. Later, when the company is bigger. Later, when there are more employees. Later, when revenue is higher. Later, when things settle down.

But later is usually when the mess is harder to fix.

The best time to build a secure AI stack is before the business is dependent on messy habits. Before customer data is scattered across too many places. Before former employees still have access to old tools. Before automations are running that nobody remembers creating. Before sensitive files are uploaded casually. Before leadership realizes it cannot explain how work moves through the company.

Early structure does not have to be heavy. It simply has to be intentional. Decide what matters. Decide who can access it. Decide which tools are approved. Decide how work is reviewed. Decide where records live. Decide how the business will respond when something goes wrong.

Those decisions create stability. They also make growth cleaner. When the business adds people, services, clients, vendors, and AI capability, it is not adding them to chaos. It is adding them to a foundation.

That is how small businesses become serious businesses without losing their soul.

The chapter in one sentence

If you remember nothing else from this chapter, remember this: AI should only move as fast as the trust structure underneath it can safely support.

The secure AI stack is not about scaring business owners. It is about giving them command. It is about knowing what the system can see, what it can do, who can use it, where the data goes, how decisions are reviewed, and how the company recovers when something breaks.

That is how AI becomes usable at scale. Not by pretending risk does not exist, and not by letting fear freeze the business in place. The answer is disciplined confidence.

Build the stack. Protect the data. Control the permissions. Choose tools carefully. Keep the records. Make recovery possible. Keep humans accountable where trust is on the line.

Then, once the foundation is secure, the next question becomes rhythm. How often does the business review what AI is doing? How does the owner stay in command without staring at dashboards all day? How does the team turn all of this into a normal operating habit instead of another project that fades after a week?

That is where we go next: the weekly AI operating rhythm.

Chapter 20
The Weekly AI Operating Rhythm

AI does not remove the need for rhythm. It makes rhythm more important.

That is one of the things many business owners miss when they first start using AI. They think the goal is to make everything faster, always on, constantly moving, and somehow self-managing. They imagine a business where the tools run, the dashboards update, the messages go out, the summaries appear, the invoices move, the content gets drafted, the customers are answered, and the owner finally gets to breathe.

And yes, AI can make a business faster. It can remove friction. It can take the repetitive work off a human plate. It can help an owner see patterns sooner, respond sooner, prepare sooner, and recover sooner. But speed without rhythm turns into noise. A business that is always moving is not automatically a business that is moving in the right direction.

This is why every AI-ready business needs a weekly operating rhythm.

Not a complicated ritual. Not another meeting that everyone dreads. Not a spreadsheet nobody updates until something breaks. I am talking about a simple, steady habit of looking at the business, checking what the systems touched, asking what changed, and deciding what needs attention before small problems become expensive ones.

The weekly rhythm is where the owner stays in command.

When I say command, I do not mean control in a harsh way. I mean awareness. I mean stewardship. I mean the owner still understands the business well enough to lead it. The AI can assist. The automation can move. The tools can organize. The dashboards can summarize. But the business still needs a human who knows what matters.

A business needs a heartbeat

Every healthy business has a rhythm, whether the owner has named it or not. There is a rhythm to sales. There is a rhythm to customers. There is a rhythm to bills, payroll, inventory, content, follow-up, service delivery, team communication, and leadership decisions. When the rhythm is clear, the business feels steadier. When the rhythm is missing, everything feels urgent.

Before AI, a messy rhythm could hide for a long time. The business owner could carry the missing structure in memory. The team could ask questions in passing. Someone could search through email. Someone could remember that a customer needed a call back. Someone could patch the process with effort, personality, and late nights.

But AI changes the pressure. Once systems begin helping with work, the business can produce more activity than the owner can casually inspect. More messages can be drafted. More customer notes can be summarized. More workflows can be triggered. More reports can be generated. More decisions can be suggested. That sounds helpful, and it can be. But it also means the business needs a scheduled way to look at what happened.

A weekly rhythm becomes the heartbeat. It gives the owner a regular moment to ask: Are we still aligned? Are our tools still helping? Are our customers being treated well? Are our people clear? Are our risks being watched? Are our decisions still human where they need to be human?

That kind of rhythm protects the business from drifting. It keeps AI from becoming an invisible force that quietly shapes the company without leadership noticing.

Start with visibility, not activity

One of the easiest mistakes in the AI era is confusing activity with progress. A tool can create twenty drafts, summarize ten conversations, organize a folder, build a report, schedule reminders, and generate a list of next steps. That can feel productive. But activity is not the same as movement toward the right outcome.

The weekly rhythm should begin with visibility. Not with a long task list. Not with panic. Not with trying to micromanage every click. The owner simply needs to see the business clearly enough to know where attention belongs.

What changed this week? What came in? What went out? What got delayed? What got escalated? What did the AI touch? What did customers experience? What did the team repeat more than once? What created confusion? What created confidence?

Those questions are simple, but they are powerful. They pull the owner out of the daily rush and back into leadership.

They also reveal something many owners do not see until they slow down: most business problems announce themselves before they become emergencies.

A customer complaint usually has a trail. A missed payment usually has a trail. A confused employee usually has a trail. A broken automation usually has a trail. A security concern usually has a trail. A bad decision usually has a trail. The issue is not always that the warning signs were invisible. The issue is that nobody had a rhythm for noticing them.

AI can help gather the signals, but the owner must decide what the signals mean.

Review what the AI touched

If a business uses AI casually, nobody may know where it was used. One employee uses it to rewrite a customer email. Another uses it to summarize a meeting. Another uses it to draft a proposal. Another uses it to analyze sales notes. Another uses it to produce social media content. None of that is automatically wrong, but unmanaged use creates blind spots.

The weekly operating rhythm gives the business a way to make AI visible without making people feel punished for using it.

This distinction matters. The goal is not to scare the team away from AI. The goal is to make sure the business knows where AI is influencing communication, decisions, customer experience, financial work, legal language, internal knowledge, and public reputation. When AI is used in small harmless ways, the review may be quick. When AI touches sensitive areas, the review needs more care.

A smart owner does not ask, Did we use AI? The better question is, Where did AI influence the business this week?

That question changes the quality of leadership. It helps the owner see whether AI is being used as a helper or as an unapproved decision-maker. It helps the team understand that AI is welcome inside the right guardrails. It helps the business catch small mistakes before they reach customers, employees, partners, or regulators.

This is especially important because AI mistakes can sound confident. A wrong answer may be written beautifully. A weak recommendation may look polished. A risky message may feel professional. That is why review cannot be based only on whether the output sounds good. It has to be based on whether it is accurate, appropriate, secure, and aligned with the business.

The weekly rhythm gives the business a place to check that.

Separate automation from judgment

A healthy AI rhythm separates the work machines can speed up from the judgment humans must protect. This is not anti-technology. It is mature technology leadership.

There are many things AI can help with safely when the process is designed well. It can organize information, summarize patterns, draft first versions, prepare checklists, surface exceptions, route routine tasks, remind people of deadlines, and help leaders see what they might miss. Those uses can create real relief.

But there are other things that should not be handed off casually. Who gets access to sensitive data? Which customer receives an exception? Which employee issue requires human care? Which financial decision affects cash flow? Which legal statement represents the company? Which security alert needs escalation? Which promise should be made publicly?

Those are not just tasks. Those are judgment points.

The weekly operating rhythm teaches the business to recognize the difference. Instead of asking, Can AI do this? the owner learns to ask, Should AI be allowed to do this without human review?

That question is one of the most important leadership questions in the AI era. It prevents the business from being impressed by capability alone. Just because a system can draft, sort, rank, recommend, or trigger does not mean it should do so without oversight. The owner is not trying to slow the company down. The owner is deciding where speed is safe and where judgment is sacred.

When a business gets that right, AI becomes calmer. The team knows what can be automated. They know what requires review. They know where to escalate. They know which decisions belong to humans. That clarity reduces fear, reduces confusion, and reduces risk.

Protect the team from tool chaos

A weekly rhythm also protects the people inside the business. This matters because AI adoption can become exhausting when every week brings a new tool, a new login, a new feature, a new integration, and a new promise that this one will finally fix everything.

Teams do not burn out only because they have too much work. They burn out because the work keeps changing shape without explanation. One week they are told to use one platform. The next week someone adds another. A process changes. A workflow moves. A customer note is stored in a different place. A report has a new format. A task gets automated, but nobody explains what happens when the automation fails.

That is not transformation. That is confusion with a subscription fee.

The weekly rhythm gives the owner a chance to ask whether the tools are actually helping the people who use them. Are we reducing friction or creating new friction? Are we saving time or moving the burden somewhere else? Are people clearer or more confused? Are we asking employees to trust systems they do not understand? Are we giving them a way to raise concerns before something breaks?

This is where leadership becomes very human. A business can be advanced and still be kind. It can be efficient and still be thoughtful. It can automate repetitive work while respecting the judgment, dignity, and lived experience of the people doing the work.

The best AI systems do not make good people feel replaceable. They make good people more effective. But that only happens when the owner designs the rhythm, not just the software.

Make trust a weekly discipline

Trust is not something a business declares once. It is something a business maintains. In the AI era, trust has to be checked regularly because the systems are moving, the data is moving, the tools are updating, and customer expectations are changing.

A weekly trust check does not need to be dramatic. It can be as simple as asking whether anything happened that could affect customer confidence, employee confidence, financial confidence, operational confidence, or security confidence. The answer may be no, and that is fine. The value is in the habit.

If something did happen, the weekly rhythm gives the business a place to respond before silence becomes a problem. Maybe a customer received the wrong message. Maybe a report pulled from outdated information. Maybe an employee used an AI tool with sensitive data because no one had explained the policy. Maybe a workflow skipped a review step. Maybe an automation worked exactly as designed, but the design was wrong.

Those moments are not failures if the business learns from them quickly. They become failures when the business ignores them, hides them, repeats them, or lets them grow.

This is one reason I believe so strongly in building businesses with audit trails, visible decisions, and secure operating layers. Not because every owner needs to become a cybersecurity expert. They do not. But every owner does need to know that trust cannot live inside a black box. If the business cannot explain what happened, who approved it, what system touched it, and how it will be prevented next time, trust becomes fragile.

A weekly rhythm strengthens that trust. It says, We are paying attention. We are learning. We are not letting speed outrun responsibility.

The owner does not need to do everything

There is one point I want to make very clearly because many business owners hear a chapter like this and immediately think it means more work for them. It does not have to.

The owner does not need to personally inspect every task, every prompt, every dashboard, every workflow, and every decision. That would defeat the purpose. The weekly AI operating rhythm is not about carrying the whole business on your back. It is about creating a leadership checkpoint that keeps the business honest.

In a small business, that rhythm may be a quiet hour once a week. In a growing company, it may become a leadership review. In a larger organization, it may become part of operations, security, compliance, customer experience, and strategy. The shape can change as the company grows. The principle stays the same.

Someone needs to look. Someone needs to ask better questions. Someone needs to notice what the systems are doing. Someone needs to decide what deserves attention. Someone needs to close the loop.

That is leadership in the AI era. Not knowing every technical detail. Not chasing every new tool. Not pretending to be a machine. Leadership is creating the conditions where the business can move fast without becoming careless.

The handoff into the future

By this point in the book, we have moved through a major shift. We have talked about speed, software, trust, data, hype, automation, fragmentation, cybersecurity, dependency, human control, the business brain, repetitive work, and the secure AI stack. All of that leads to this practical truth: AI-ready businesses do not run on excitement. They run on rhythm.

The weekly rhythm is what turns ideas into operating behavior. It is where the owner stops treating AI as a novelty and starts treating it as part of the business foundation. It is where the company learns to ask what changed, what worked, what failed, what needs review, and what needs to improve.

This is how an ordinary business begins to become extraordinary. Not by acting like a giant corporation. Not by buying every tool. Not by trying to sound futuristic. It becomes extraordinary by building a calm, clear, trustworthy way to operate in a faster world.

And once that rhythm exists, the next question becomes unavoidable.

What kind of team can thrive inside it?

That is where the future of work really begins. Because the AI-ready business is not only built with better systems. It is built with people who know how to think, adapt, question, collaborate, and lead alongside machines without losing what makes them human.

Part Five - The Future

Chapter 21

The Team of the Future

The team of the future is not made of people who act like machines. It is made of people who know how to work with machines without becoming smaller than them.

That distinction matters. Because when people first hear about AI in business, the conversation almost always turns into a fear conversation. Will AI take the jobs? Will people be replaced? Will companies need fewer employees? Will everyone have to become technical? Will human work still matter?

But the mistake is believing the future belongs to the machine alone.

It does not.

The future belongs to businesses that know how to combine machine speed with human judgment. And that means the team of the future is not less human. It has to become more human on purpose.

The old team model was built for slower systems

For a long time, businesses organized teams around access to information. One person knew the customer history. One person knew the payroll process. One person knew where the files were. One person knew which spreadsheet mattered. One person knew how to pull the report. One person knew the password, the vendor, the exception, the workaround, or the secret little process that kept everything moving.

AI exposes that old model. It does not always break it immediately, but it makes the weakness harder to ignore. When a business wants to move faster, answer faster, serve customers faster, make better decisions, and protect itself better, it can no longer depend on knowledge trapped in individual heads.

This does not mean people become less important. It means the way people contribute has to mature.

The team of the future cannot be valuable only because one person knows where something is hidden. The team of the future becomes valuable because people know how to think, interpret, care, connect, judge, improve, and lead the systems around them.

That is a better kind of value. It is not built on hoarding information. It is built on wisdom, communication, ownership, and trust.

AI changes the employee bargain

In the old workplace, many employees were rewarded for doing repetitive work reliably. They copied information from one place to another. They answered the same questions. They rebuilt the same reports. They checked the same boxes. They chased the same approvals. They fixed the same preventable mistakes. They carried the weight of business inefficiency because the company had no better system.

AI challenges that bargain. If a machine can draft the first version, summarize the meeting, organize the notes, route the task, flag the exception, or produce the report, then the human role has to move higher.

That can feel threatening when it is handled badly. If leadership introduces AI as a replacement strategy, people protect themselves. They hide their work. They resist new tools. They stop sharing ideas. They worry that the more efficient they become, the less needed they will be.

That fear is not irrational. It is a leadership problem.

A responsible business owner has to frame AI differently. AI should not be introduced as a way to make people invisible. It should be introduced as a way to stop wasting human life on work that never needed a human soul in the first place.

People should not spend their best energy searching through broken folders, rewriting the same message, rebuilding reports that should have generated automatically, or acting as human duct tape between disconnected systems. That is not noble work. That is expensive exhaustion.

The team of the future still works hard, but the work shifts. Less copying. More checking. Less chasing. More deciding. Less searching. More understanding. Less pretending that busy equals valuable. More contribution that actually moves the business forward.

The most valuable people will be translators

Every AI-ready business needs translators. I do not mean language translators, although that may also matter. I mean people who can translate between the business need, the customer reality, the tool capability, and the human consequence.

That person is not just using AI. That person is translating meaning.

The translator does not need to be the most technical person in the room. They need to be observant. They need to understand the business. They need to care about outcomes. They need enough comfort with AI to ask better questions, and enough human sense to know when the answer is incomplete.

In a small business, the owner may be the translator at first. In a growing company, this skill may show up in operations, customer success, finance, HR, marketing, security, or leadership. The job title matters less than the ability.

The businesses that win will not only hire people who can click buttons. They will develop people who can connect dots.

Curiosity becomes a business skill

In the AI era, curiosity is no longer a cute personality trait. It is a business skill.

Curious people ask why the process exists. They ask what the customer actually needed. They ask what the data is missing. They ask why the tool made that recommendation. They ask what happens if the system fails. They ask who is affected by a decision. They ask whether the faster way is also the better way.

That kind of curiosity protects a company.

A team without curiosity becomes overly dependent on instructions. They wait to be told what to do. They trust the output because the system produced it. They repeat the process because that is how it was set up. They do not question whether the work still makes sense.

That is dangerous in a machine-speed world.

The team of the future has to be willing to question without becoming difficult. There is a difference. A difficult person creates friction for attention. A curious person creates clarity for the business. They are not trying to slow everyone down. They are trying to make sure the company does not run quickly in the wrong direction.

This is why culture matters so much. If employees are punished for asking questions, they will stop asking. If they are embarrassed for not understanding a new tool immediately, they will pretend. If they are told that AI is perfect, they will either distrust leadership or stop trusting themselves.

A strong business creates room for intelligent questions. It teaches people that asking, checking, and escalating are signs of professionalism, not weakness.

The manager becomes a coach of judgment

AI also changes management. The manager of the future cannot simply assign tasks and monitor completion. Some of the tasks will be automated. Some will be assisted. Some will be suggested by systems. Some will move before a manager sees every step.

That means managers have to become coaches of judgment.

They need to help people understand what good looks like. They need to explain where AI can help and where it cannot decide alone. They need to define what requires review. They need to create safe escalation paths. They need to help employees develop confidence without becoming careless.

This is a much more mature form of leadership than simply asking, Did you finish it?

A manager now has to ask, Was the output accurate? Was the customer treated well? Was the right information used? Was anything sensitive exposed? Did the tool make an assumption? Did we review the judgment point? Did the process create trust?

Those questions turn management into stewardship. They also reveal which leaders are ready for the AI era and which leaders are only comfortable supervising motion.

The best managers will not compete with AI by trying to be faster than software. They will become better at developing people who can use software wisely.

Do not build a team that is afraid of the tools

Fear is one of the fastest ways to ruin AI adoption. Not healthy caution. Not security awareness. Not ethical care. I mean fear that makes people freeze, hide, or pretend.

Some business owners unintentionally create that fear. They announce a new AI tool without explaining why. They make big statements about efficiency without saying how people will be protected. They shame employees who are slower to learn. They allow one tech-savvy person to become the gatekeeper while everyone else feels behind.

That approach may create compliance, but it does not create capability.

The team of the future needs training that feels practical, not intimidating. People need permission to learn. They need clear rules. They need examples that connect to their actual work. They need to understand what information should never be pasted into an outside tool. They need to know when AI-generated content must be reviewed. They need to know who to ask when something feels off.

Most people do not need a lecture on artificial intelligence. They need confidence using AI responsibly inside their role.

When people feel safe learning, they become useful faster. When they understand the guardrails, they make fewer risky choices. When they see that AI is meant to remove low-value friction instead of erase their worth, they are more willing to participate honestly.

Trust your people, but design the system

There is a phrase I believe every business owner should remember: do not use trust as a substitute for design.

You can trust your people and still build controls. You can respect your team and still require review. You can believe someone has good intentions and still limit access to sensitive information. You can appreciate speed and still create approval points.

That is not suspicion. That is good business.

The AI era requires this balance because mistakes can scale. A confusing instruction can produce many confusing outputs. A bad permission setting can expose too much data. An unchecked automation can repeat the same error quickly.

A polished AI message can reach customers before anyone realizes it created the wrong expectation.

The answer is not to distrust everyone. The answer is to design a system that helps good people do good work safely.

That means roles must be clearer. Access must be intentional. Sensitive work must have review. AI use must be visible where it matters. The team must know the difference between a draft, a recommendation, and a decision. The business must make it easy to do the right thing and harder to accidentally do the risky thing.

This is where the future team becomes stronger than the old team. The old team often depended on heroic effort. The future team depends on intelligent structure.

The human advantage is not disappearing

The more capable AI becomes, the more tempting it is to underestimate people. That is a mistake.

AI can process information quickly. It can generate options. It can summarize, draft, compare, predict, and organize. But business is not only information processing. Business is trust between people. It is judgment under pressure. It is knowing when a customer needs patience instead of policy. It is understanding when a team member is struggling. It is recognizing the difference between a profitable decision and a wise one.

AI can support those moments, but it cannot fully own them.

The human advantage is context, conscience, relationship, imagination, courage, and care. Those words may sound soft until you run a real business. Then you learn they are not soft at all. They are the difference between a company people tolerate and a company people trust.

The team of the future must protect that advantage. Not by rejecting technology, but by refusing to become numb inside it.

A business that uses AI well should become more responsive, not colder. More organized, not more robotic. More secure, not more paranoid. More efficient, not more careless. More scalable, not less human.

That is the standard.

The new hiring question

As AI changes work, hiring has to change too. Business owners will still need skills, experience, reliability, and professionalism. But they will also need to look for something deeper.

Can this person learn? Can this person think with tools without surrendering judgment to them? Can this person communicate clearly? Can this person handle change without creating drama? Can this person protect trust? Can this person see the human being behind the workflow?

Those questions matter because the future team will not be static. Tools will change. Processes will change. Customer expectations will change. Security risks will change. The business model may change. A person who can only follow yesterday instructions may struggle. A person who can learn, question, adapt, and care can grow with the company.

This does not mean every employee has to be a visionary. Businesses still need dependable people who do steady work. But dependability in the AI era includes a willingness to learn. It includes honesty when something is unclear. It includes care with data. It includes respect for the system and enough confidence to speak up when the system gets something wrong.

The best teams will be built from people who are both teachable and trustworthy.

The future is a leadership decision

The team of the future will not appear by accident. It has to be built.

Business owners have to decide what kind of workplace they are creating. Are they using AI to squeeze people harder, or to remove friction so people can do better work? Are they building a culture of fear, or a culture of responsible confidence? Are they hiding decisions inside systems, or making accountability clearer? Are they treating employees as replaceable costs, or as human intelligence amplified by better tools?

Those decisions will shape the business more than any single platform.

Because at the end of the day, AI does not create the culture. Leadership does. AI does not define the standard. Leadership does. AI does not decide whether people feel safe enough to learn, honest enough to question, and responsible enough to protect the customer. Leadership does.

This is why the next chapter matters. The team of the future needs a different kind of leader. Not a leader who knows every answer. Not a leader who chases every trend. Not a leader who pretends machines have removed the need for wisdom.

The AI-ready leader is calmer than that. Clearer than that. More disciplined than that.

And in the invisible war for trust, speed, and survival, that kind of leadership may become the greatest competitive advantage of all.

Part Five - The Future

Chapter 22
The AI-Ready Leader

The AI-ready leader is not the person who knows every tool first. It is the person who knows what should never be surrendered to a tool.

That may sound simple, but it is one of the most important distinctions in modern business. We have entered a season where leaders are being pressured from every direction. Move faster. Automate more. Adopt the newest platform. Cut costs. Increase output. Personalize everything. Respond instantly. Build smarter systems. Do not fall behind.

AI does not remove the need for leadership. It exposes the quality of it.

The AI-ready leader is not louder than everyone else. They are not necessarily the most technical person in the room. They are not chasing every shiny promise. They are clear. They are calm. They are curious. They know how to ask better questions. They know how to protect the human center of the business while still pushing the business forward.

That kind of leader is going to matter more than ever.

Leadership begins with clarity

AI loves unclear environments because unclear environments create endless activity. If a business does not know what it values, AI can still generate content. If a company does not know its customer, AI can still write messages. If a team does not understand its priorities, AI can still produce reports, tasks, summaries, and dashboards.

But activity is not leadership.

The first responsibility of an AI-ready leader is clarity. Not perfect certainty. Clarity. The team needs to know what the business is trying to protect, who it serves, what standard matters, what can move quickly, and what must slow down for review.

Without that clarity, AI becomes a very fast assistant to a very confused organization. It will help people do more of what they already do, even if what they already do is wasteful, disconnected, or misaligned. It will make the noise sound more polished. It will make unfinished thinking look presentable. It will give a weak decision a professional tone.

That is dangerous because polished confusion can be harder to challenge than messy confusion. When something looks organized, people assume someone thought it through. In the AI era, that assumption will not always be safe.

A leader has to define the frame before the tools start filling it. What problem are we solving? What outcome matters? Who owns the decision? What information is reliable? What risk are we accepting? What promise are we making to the customer? What should never happen in the name of speed?

Those questions are not technical. They are leadership questions. They are also the difference between using AI as leverage and letting AI amplify disorder.

The leader does not need to know every prompt

A lot of business owners quietly disqualify themselves from the AI conversation because they think they are not technical enough. They hear people talk about models, tokens, agents, workflows, APIs, integrations, and automation logic, and they think, maybe this is not my world.

That is understandable, but it is also a trap.

The AI-ready leader does not need to become a software engineer to lead an AI-ready business. They do need to understand enough to ask intelligent questions, set boundaries, and recognize when a tool is being treated like magic instead of infrastructure.

The leader has to be fluent enough to govern.

That means learning the language of outcomes, risk, access, review, reliability, and accountability. It means being able to say, explain how this works in plain English. It means being willing to ask, where does the data go? Who can see it? What happens if it is wrong? What does the human review? How do we undo it? What record is kept? What customer expectation does this create?

Those are not beginner questions. Those are grown-up questions.

Calm becomes a competitive advantage

AI creates urgency. Some of that urgency is useful. Businesses should pay attention. They should learn. They should experiment. They should modernize. They should not pretend the world is standing still.

But panic is not strategy.

The AI-ready leader has to be calm enough to distinguish movement from progress. Calm enough to avoid buying tools just because a competitor mentioned them. Calm enough to stop a workflow that is creating risk. Calm enough to tell the team that not every task should be automated. Calm enough to admit that the company needs a better foundation before adding another layer of intelligence.

That is what modern customers want more than most companies realize. They want responsiveness, but they also want confidence. They want convenience, but they also want care. They want speed, but they do not want to feel like they are being processed by a company that forgot there is a person on the other side.

The AI-ready leader protects that balance.

The new leadership skill is asking better questions

The AI-ready leader earns authority by asking better questions.

What are we assuming? What is the tool optimizing for? What did it leave out? Who benefits from this workflow? Who might be harmed by it? What information are we trusting? What part of this decision needs a human being? What would make this feel fair to the customer? What would make this unsafe? What would we need to see before we scale it?

Questions like that slow down the right things. They do not slow the business down everywhere. They slow the business down at the judgment point, where one careless decision can create a larger problem later.

That is not anti-innovation. That is how innovation survives contact with reality.

A leader must protect the promise of the business

AI can help a business deliver those promises more consistently. It can remind, route, summarize, flag, organize, and support. It can make it easier for a small team to show up like a larger company. It can help a business stay responsive even when demand grows.

But AI can also accidentally rewrite the promise if no one is watching.

A chatbot can promise something the business cannot deliver. An automated email can sound colder than the brand ever intended. A recommendation system can steer customers based on incomplete data. A workflow can prioritize speed over sensitivity. A generated policy can sound official without reflecting the company values.

The AI-ready leader understands that the brand is not just the logo, the website, or the sales page. The brand is the pattern of trust people experience over time. If AI changes that pattern, the business changes, whether leadership meant to or not.

That is why leaders must protect the promise. They must define what the company sounds like, what it will not say, what it will not automate without review, what kind of customer experience it refuses to sacrifice, and what human moments still deserve human attention.

The AI-ready leader learns the difference.

Accountability cannot be automated away

One of the biggest mistakes a business can make is treating AI like a place to hide responsibility. The system sent it. The tool recommended it. The automation did it. The model generated it. The vendor configured it. The platform allowed it.

None of those explanations remove ownership from the business.

The business remains accountable.

The AI-ready leader accepts this before anything goes wrong. They do not wait for a crisis to ask who owns the decision. They define accountability while the system is being designed. They make sure important outputs can be reviewed. They make sure sensitive actions are logged. They make sure the team knows when to escalate. They make sure vendors do not become invisible decision-makers inside the company.

This is not about fear. It is about maturity.

A mature leader can say, we will use powerful tools, and we will own how we use them. We will benefit from speed, and we will remain responsible for the result. We will automate parts of the process, and we will not automate away our conscience.

That statement may never appear in a policy document, but it needs to live in the way the company operates.

The leader sets the learning temperature

An AI-ready leader sets a better temperature.

They make learning normal. They admit when something is new. They separate curiosity from incompetence. They give people permission to say, I do not understand this yet. They create practical training instead of dramatic announcements. They reinforce that responsible use matters more than appearing impressive.

A good leader does not ignore those feelings. A good leader gives the team a stronger story.

The story is not, AI is coming for you. The story is, we are going to learn how to use better tools so we can stop wasting talent on work that drains us and start protecting the work that makes us valuable.

That story creates participation. It creates honesty. It creates a culture where people can improve without pretending. And in the AI era, the companies that can learn honestly will outperform the companies that only perform confidence.

Leadership is the guardrail around speed

Speed is going to be one of the defining pressures of the next decade. Customers will expect faster responses. Competitors will launch faster. Markets will shift faster. Tools will evolve faster. Decisions will stack faster.

The answer is not to become reckless. The answer is to build leadership that can hold speed without being consumed by it.

That means leaders must know where the business can move quickly and where it cannot. Drafting can be fast. Final approval may need review. Research can be fast. Strategy may need discussion. Routing can be fast. Sensitive decisions may need human oversight. Customer support can be assisted. Customer trust still has to be earned.

The leader is the guardrail around speed because the leader defines the difference between acceleration and danger.

The AI-ready leader is not trying to make the company slow. They are trying to make the company strong enough to move fast without falling apart.

That is the real leadership challenge now.

The leader of the future is deeply human

There is a strange irony in this moment. The more advanced the tools become, the more human leadership has to become.

Not softer. Not weaker. More human.

That is not a small responsibility.

The AI-ready leader does not try to out-machine the machine. They become more disciplined in the things machines cannot fully replace: courage, discernment, humility, empathy, accountability, and vision.

Those qualities are not decorations. They are operational assets. Courage will stop a bad system before it scales. Humility will listen when an employee says something is wrong. Empathy will notice when efficiency is damaging the customer experience. Accountability will own the outcome instead of hiding behind technology.

That is leadership in the AI era.

Prepare before pressure arrives

The worst time to decide your AI principles is during a crisis. The worst time to define human review is after the wrong message has gone out. The worst time to clarify accountability is after a customer asks who approved the decision. The worst time to train the team is after someone has pasted sensitive information into the wrong place.

The AI-ready leader prepares before pressure arrives.

They make the company learn while the stakes are manageable. They test tools before trusting them. They document the important decisions. They create simple rules for data, approvals, and review. They build a culture where people know that raising a concern is part of the job, not an interruption of it.

Preparation is not glamorous, but it is powerful. It is the reason one company stays steady while another company panics. It is the reason one team knows what to do while another team waits for the owner to put out every fire.

This is where the invisible war becomes very real. The battle is not only over who has the newest AI tool. It is over who has the leadership maturity to use the tool well.

The next chapter moves into that pressure directly. Because the AI-ready leader is not leading in a quiet world. They are leading against companies that are learning to move faster, serve faster, decide faster, and scale faster.

The question is not whether your business can keep up with every trend.

The question is whether your business can become clear, trustworthy, and disciplined enough to compete at the new speed of the market.

Part Five - The Future

Chapter 23

Competing Against Companies That Move Faster

The company that scares you most in the AI era may not be bigger than you. It may simply be moving with less drag.

That is the part many business owners miss. They look at competition through the old lens. Bigger office. Bigger staff. Bigger budget. Bigger marketing department. Bigger technology team. Bigger everything. And for a long time, that was a reasonable way to think. Size created reach. Size created capacity. Size created options.

But AI has changed the math of movement. A small team can now write faster, research faster, respond faster, analyze faster, build faster, test faster, and follow up faster than businesses that used to have a much larger advantage. A two-person company with a clean operating rhythm can sometimes feel more responsive than a twenty-person company drowning in meetings, scattered tools, and slow approvals.

That does not mean size no longer matters. Resources still matter. Capital still matters. Distribution still matters. Relationships still matter. But speed has become more available. And once speed becomes more available, the real question becomes whether the business is organized enough to use it.

This is where the invisible war becomes a market war. It is not only a fight for attention. It is a fight for trust, timing, execution, and follow-through. The businesses that learn faster will adjust faster. The businesses that adjust faster will serve faster. The businesses that serve faster, while still protecting quality and trust, will become difficult to ignore.

That is the pressure every modern business owner is walking into.

Speed is not the same as rushing

Before we go any further, we have to make an important distinction. Moving faster is not the same as rushing.

Rushing is frantic. Rushing skips judgment. Rushing sends the email before anyone checks whether it is true. Rushing signs up for tools without understanding what they touch. Rushing lets the loudest trend dictate the business strategy. Rushing is what happens when urgency is not disciplined by leadership.

Real speed is different. Real speed comes from clarity. It comes from fewer handoffs, cleaner data, better decisions, trusted processes, and a team that knows what to do without asking the same question fifteen times. Real speed feels calm on the outside because the inside has structure.

Customers can feel the difference. A rushed business feels sloppy. A fast business feels responsive. A rushed business creates anxiety. A fast business creates confidence. A rushed business makes mistakes and calls them innovation. A fast business learns, improves, and keeps its promises.

The goal is not to become the business that says yes to everything, replies without thinking, and automates every touchpoint until the customer feels like a ticket number. The goal is to become the business that removes unnecessary delay while protecting the moments where judgment matters.

That is the kind of speed worth building.

The new competitor may not look like a competitor

In the old world, competitors were easy to identify. They had a storefront like yours. They advertised in the same area. They served the same customers. They attended the same local events. You knew who they were because they looked like you.

In the AI era, that will not always be true.

Your competitor may be a business in another city with a stronger online process. It may be a solo operator who uses AI to produce the output of a small department. It may be a company that does not have better talent than you, but has a better follow-up system. It may be a new brand that has not been around long, but responds faster, explains better, organizes information better, and makes the customer feel more guided.

That is uncomfortable, but it is also clarifying. Competition is no longer only about who has the same service. It is about who creates the better experience around the service.

A customer does not always know how hard the work is behind the scenes. They know whether you answered. They know whether you made the next step clear. They know whether your proposal was understandable. They know whether the payment process was easy. They know whether your team sounded coordinated. They know whether you remembered what they told you last time.

AI gives businesses more ways to improve those details. That means the market will become less forgiving of avoidable friction. Not because customers are mean, but because they will increasingly experience businesses that make things easier.

Once customers experience easier, confusing starts to feel expensive.

The advantage of a clean business

A clean business has an advantage now. Not perfect. Clean.

A clean business knows where its information lives. It knows what happens when a lead comes in. It knows who approves what. It knows which work should be automated and which work should stay human. It knows how customer data is handled. It knows which tools matter and which tools are creating noise.

That kind of cleanliness used to feel like administrative discipline. Now it is competitive strategy.

AI performs better in clean environments. Automation performs better in clean environments. Teams perform better in clean environments. Customers feel better in clean environments, even if they never see the backend. The business simply moves with less hesitation because people are not constantly searching, guessing, retyping, correcting, or rebuilding what already exists somewhere else.

This is why fragmented tools become so expensive. They do not only cost subscription fees. They cost timing. They cost confidence. They cost trust. They make simple questions harder to answer. They make the business feel slower than it really is.

The companies that move faster are often not doing magic. They are doing fewer unnecessary things. They are reducing the distance between information and action. They are making it easier for the right person, or the right system, to know what needs to happen next.

That is not glamorous, but it wins.

Small businesses are not powerless

One of the reasons I care so much about this conversation is because many smaller business owners hear about AI and immediately feel behind. They imagine large companies with huge technology budgets, full data teams, consultants, legal departments, cybersecurity staff, and internal innovation labs. Then they look at their own business and think, how am I supposed to compete with that?

That question is honest. But it is not the whole truth.

Large companies have advantages, but they also have drag. More meetings. More approvals. More legacy systems. More politics. More departments that have to agree before anything changes. More tools that were bought years ago and never fully integrated. More people protecting the old way because the old way is familiar.

A smaller business can sometimes move with more courage because the distance between decision and action is shorter. The owner can see the problem, decide the standard, adjust the process, and test the improvement without waiting for six committees to bless common sense.

That does not mean small businesses should be careless. It means they should not underestimate the advantage of being close to the work.

Closeness matters. You know the customer pain. You hear the complaints. You see where the team struggles. You know which tasks drain time. You know which promises matter. You know which moments require care. AI can help you act on that knowledge faster, but your closeness is still the source of the wisdom.

The future does not only belong to the biggest companies. It belongs to the companies that can learn quickly without losing themselves.

Do not compete on noise

When the market speeds up, many businesses respond by making more noise. More posts. More emails. More offers. More content. More promotions. More announcements. More everything.

AI makes that easier. It can generate more words than any business could reasonably publish. It can create campaigns, captions, scripts, articles, sales pages, follow-up messages, and presentations in minutes. Used well, that is helpful. Used carelessly, it becomes a fog machine.

The future customer is going to be surrounded by generated noise. They will see more content, not less. They will receive more messages, not less. They will be targeted, retargeted, reminded, nudged, segmented, and personalized until personalization itself starts to feel ordinary.

That means noise will not be enough.

A business that wants to compete at machine speed cannot only produce more. It has to mean more. It has to be clearer. It has to be more useful. It has to be more trustworthy. It has to sound like a human business with a real point of view, not a machine trying to fill a calendar.

This is good news for thoughtful leaders. The more generic the market becomes, the more valuable real clarity becomes. The more automated communication becomes, the more powerful honest communication becomes. The more crowded the feed becomes, the more customers will notice a business that actually understands their problem.

So yes, use AI to communicate faster. But do not let it flatten your voice, your values, or your judgment. Compete on usefulness, not volume. Compete on trust, not noise.

The company with the better learning loop wins

In a slow market, a business can sometimes survive for years on old assumptions. The customer still wants this. The process still works. The message still lands. The team still understands the priority. The competitor is still doing what they did last year.

In a fast market, old assumptions expire quietly.

The businesses that win will not be the ones that guessed right once. They will be the ones that keep learning. They will notice when customers stop responding. They will see when a workflow is creating delays. They will listen when employees say the tool is causing more work than it saves. They will review what AI is producing instead of assuming more output means better outcomes.

This is the learning loop. Observe. Decide. Act. Review. Adjust. Then do it again.

AI can strengthen that loop. It can surface patterns, summarize feedback, compare performance, flag recurring problems, and help teams see what used to hide inside the daily mess. But the loop still needs leadership. Someone has to care enough to ask what the data means. Someone has to decide what standard matters. Someone has to be willing to change the process when the evidence says the old one is not working.

A company that learns weekly will eventually outperform a company that only reacts quarterly. A company that pays attention will eventually outperform a company that waits for a crisis to reveal what everyone already felt.

That is how speed becomes durable. Not because the business never makes mistakes, but because the business does not let mistakes sit unexamined.

Protect what makes you hard to copy

AI will make many things easier to copy. A competitor can study your website. They can imitate your tone. They can generate similar content. They can build a decent-looking brand faster than ever. They can create proposals, training materials, and customer sequences that look professional from the outside.

But they cannot easily copy earned trust. They cannot copy your lived experience. They cannot copy the relationships you have built over years. They cannot copy the way you notice what matters in a customer conversation. They cannot copy your standards unless you abandon them first.

This is where business owners have to be careful. Sometimes, in the rush to modernize, they automate the very things that made customers choose them in the first place. The personal explanation becomes a generic template. The careful review becomes an instant response. The thoughtful onboarding becomes a sequence nobody has read. The founder voice becomes a polished paragraph that could belong to anybody.

Do not hand away the parts of the business that make it hard to replace.

Use AI to support those parts. Use it to prepare, organize, remind, summarize, draft, and strengthen. But keep your eye on the difference between leverage and replacement. The goal is not to become invisible inside your own business. The goal is to make the business stronger because your judgment is built into the system.

That is how a company competes against faster companies without becoming a weaker version of them.

Speed must serve the promise

Every business should ask one question before adopting a faster way of working: faster toward what?

Faster toward confusion is not progress. Faster toward sloppy service is not progress. Faster toward more content nobody trusts is not progress. Faster toward exhausted employees is not progress. Faster toward decisions no one can explain is not progress.

Speed becomes valuable when it serves the promise of the business. If your promise is care, speed should make care easier to deliver. If your promise is expertise, speed should help you prepare better, not pretend faster. If your promise is protection, speed should help you see risk sooner. If your promise is simplicity, speed should remove friction instead of adding another layer of confusion.

This is where leaders have to be honest. Some companies do not have a speed problem. They have a promise problem. They do not know what experience they are trying to create, so every tool looks useful and every trend feels urgent.

A clear promise gives speed direction. It tells the business what to automate, what to protect, what to improve, and what to leave alone. It keeps AI from becoming a collection of disconnected tricks. It turns the technology into part of the operating model.

That is how the strongest companies will compete in the AI era. They will not only move faster. They will move faster in the right direction.

The next chapter is about trust at that speed

Competing against faster companies does not mean copying their pace blindly. It means building a business that can respond, learn, decide, and serve at modern speed without losing the trust that made the business valuable.

That is not easy. It requires discipline. It requires clean systems. It requires leadership. It requires a team that understands the difference between automation and abdication. It requires the owner to stop seeing AI as a side experiment and start seeing it as part of how the business operates.

But it is possible. More than that, it is necessary.

The market is not going to slow down so every business can catch its breath. Customers are not going to forget what better service feels like. Competitors are not going to stop learning. Tools are not going to become less capable. The old pace is not coming back.

The opportunity is to build a company that does not panic in that reality. A company that moves with clarity. A company that learns honestly. A company that uses AI to remove drag while protecting judgment. A company that can be fast and still feel safe.

Because in a machine-speed world, trust does not become less important.

It becomes the reason speed works.

Part Five - The Future

Chapter 24

Building Trust in a Machine-Speed World

Speed can get attention. Trust is what keeps it.

That is one of the most important truths a business owner can carry into the AI era. The world is getting faster. Customers are moving faster. Teams are communicating faster. Tools are producing faster. Decisions are being made with more data, more automation, and less patience for old delays. But no matter how fast business becomes, people still hesitate when they do not trust what is in front of them.

A customer may love convenience, but they still want to know their information is safe. An employee may appreciate automation, but they still want to know the system will not make them look foolish. A leader may want faster reporting, but they still need confidence that the numbers mean what they appear to mean. A partner may admire innovation, but they still want to know the company behind it can be counted on.

This is why trust becomes more valuable, not less valuable, as AI becomes more common. When everything speeds up, people look for something steady. When everyone can generate polished words, people look for proof. When every business claims to be smarter, faster, and more advanced, customers begin asking a quieter question: can I believe you?

That question will shape the next era of business.

The trust gap is widening

AI creates a strange tension. On one hand, it gives businesses more power to serve people well. A company can respond quickly, summarize complex information, personalize service, identify risks earlier, and remove friction that used to frustrate customers. Used with care, AI can make a business feel more thoughtful, not less.

On the other hand, AI also gives businesses more power to appear trustworthy without actually being trustworthy. It can polish weak promises. It can make thin expertise sound confident. It can create impressive materials that hide messy operations. It can help a company sound organized even when the backend is chaos.

Customers are already learning this difference. They are learning that a clean website does not always mean a clean company. A fast reply does not always mean a real answer. A confident statement does not always mean someone checked the facts. A personalized message does not always mean anyone actually knows them.

That is the trust gap. Technology improves the surface faster than many businesses improve the substance. The companies that close that gap will earn a powerful advantage. The companies that widen it will eventually be exposed by their own speed.

Because when a business moves slowly, mistakes can hide for a while. When a business moves at machine speed, mistakes spread quickly. A bad automation can touch every customer. A wrong data field can repeat across every report.

A careless message can go out at scale. A weak security habit can become a company-wide vulnerability.

Speed amplifies whatever is already inside the business. If the business has discipline, speed amplifies discipline. If the business has confusion, speed amplifies confusion. If the business has trust, speed carries trust farther. If the business has shortcuts, speed makes the shortcuts visible.

Trust has to be engineered into the work

Many people talk about trust as if it is only a feeling. It is partly a feeling, of course. Customers feel whether a business is steady. Employees feel whether leadership is honest. Partners feel whether commitments are reliable. But in a machine-speed world, trust cannot only live in tone, personality, or intention.

Trust has to be engineered into the work.

That does not mean turning the business into something cold or mechanical. It means designing the business so the right things happen even when the day is busy, the team is tired, the inbox is full, and the pressure is high. It means making trust visible in the way information is handled, decisions are reviewed, promises are documented, and responsibilities are assigned.

A trustworthy business does not simply say, we care about your data. It knows who has access to the data. It knows where the data lives. It knows what the tools can see. It knows how long records are kept. It knows what happens when someone leaves the company. It knows how to respond when something goes wrong.

A trustworthy business does not simply say, we use AI responsibly. It knows what AI is allowed to do, what it is not allowed to do, where human approval is required, and how outputs are reviewed before they affect customers, money, contracts, safety, reputation, or people.

A trustworthy business does not simply say, our team is aligned. It has a shared operating rhythm. It has clear decision standards. It has one source of truth for important information. It does not make every employee guess which document, chat thread, spreadsheet, or memory is correct.

That is what I mean by engineering trust. It is not about removing humanity from business. It is about protecting humanity from disorder.

Customers can feel operational trust

Most customers cannot see your internal systems. They do not know what software you use. They do not know how your automations are built. They do not know whether your team has a clean workflow or a messy one. But they can feel the outcome.

They can also feel the opposite.

They can feel when the business is guessing. They can feel when the left hand does not know what the right hand promised. They can feel when automation sends a message that does not fit the situation. They can feel when a company is moving fast but not paying attention.

In the AI era, those feelings matter. Customers may not use words like operating layer or secure stack or workflow governance. They may simply say, this company is easy to work with. Or they may say, I do not know, something feels off.

That feeling is not small. It is often the difference between a sale and a lost opportunity, a renewal and a cancellation, a referral and silence.

A machine-speed business has to respect the small moments because small moments now happen at scale.

Transparency becomes a leadership skill

As AI becomes part of everyday business, leaders will need a healthier relationship with transparency. Not performative transparency, where a company says a lot without meaning much. Real transparency, where people understand what is happening, what the limits are, and who is accountable.

Customers do not need every technical detail. Most employees do not need every technical detail. But people do need enough clarity to trust the process. They need to know when they are interacting with automation. They need to know when a human will review something important. They need to know how their information is being used. They need to know where to go when something does not feel right.

Transparency does not make a business look weaker. Done correctly, it makes the business look more mature.

A leader who says, here is where we use AI, here is where we do not, here is where human judgment stays in control, and here is how we protect your information, is not behind. That leader is building confidence. That leader is showing that the company has thought beyond excitement and into responsibility.

This matters inside the company too. Employees should not feel like AI is something being quietly dropped into their work without explanation. They should understand the purpose. They should understand the boundaries. They should understand how AI helps them and where they are still expected to use judgment. They should know that leadership is not using AI as an excuse to ignore expertise, overload the team, or erase accountability.

Trust breaks when people feel managed by a system they do not understand. Trust grows when people understand the system, understand the standard, and understand their role within it.

Do not let polish replace proof

One of the dangers of AI is that it makes polish cheap. A business can create a beautiful report, a professional proposal, an impressive strategy document, a confident sales script, and a steady stream of content with very little time. That can be useful. It can also be dangerous.

Polish is not proof.

A polished answer is not automatically a correct answer. A polished policy is not automatically a practiced policy. A polished brand is not automatically a trustworthy business. A polished AI output is not automatically a responsible decision.

Leaders have to teach their teams to look past the surface. Does the information match the facts? Does the recommendation fit the customer? Does the report connect to real data? Does the message sound like the company? Does the automation respect the situation? Does the system have permission to use what it is using?

These questions may seem simple, but they are powerful. They keep AI from turning confidence into carelessness. They remind the business that speed still needs evidence. They protect the company from mistaking presentation for performance.

That question is not resistance. It is protection.

Trust with employees matters just as much

A business cannot build customer trust while destroying internal trust. The two are connected. If employees do not trust the systems, the strategy, or the leadership, that distrust eventually reaches the customer experience.

When AI enters a workplace, people often wonder what it means for them. They may not say it out loud. They may smile in the meeting. They may nod when the new tool is introduced. But inside, they are asking: will this replace me, monitor me, expose me, overload me, or make decisions about me?

A wise leader does not ignore those questions. A wise leader answers them with honesty and structure.

AI should make good employees stronger. It should reduce repetitive drain, improve access to information, support better decisions, and help people focus on work that actually requires human ability. It should not become a silent pressure machine that demands more output without more clarity.

Trust grows when employees see that AI is being introduced with standards. They know what is expected.

They know what will be measured. They know where human judgment matters. They know how mistakes will be handled. They know leadership is not pretending every tool is perfect just because it is new.

If you want a fast company, build a trustworthy company first.

The standard has to be visible

Trust also depends on standards. Not vague values printed on a wall, but standards people can actually use.

A business needs to know what good looks like. What does a responsible AI-assisted answer look like? What kind of customer information should never be pasted into a public tool? What decisions require human approval? What errors must be reported immediately? What promises can automation make, and what promises must only come from a person?

When the standard is invisible, people improvise. One employee uses AI carefully. Another uses it casually. One department checks outputs. Another publishes them directly. One manager protects customer data. Another uploads sensitive files because the tool seemed convenient. That inconsistency becomes risk.

Visible standards turn trust into a shared practice. They give people a way to move quickly without guessing. They make it easier to train new employees. They make it easier to correct mistakes without shaming people. They create a common language around what the business will and will not do.

In a machine-speed world, standards cannot live only in the founder mind. They have to move into the operating system of the business. They have to show up in onboarding, workflows, approvals, documentation, tool settings, customer communication, and leadership reviews.

That is how trust becomes repeatable.

Aetis as a trust example, not a sales pitch

This is one of the reasons I think about Aetis the way I do. Not as another app in a crowded market, but as a response to a deeper problem: businesses are being asked to move faster while also becoming harder to protect, harder to coordinate, and harder to trust.

The answer cannot simply be more tools. More tools often create more places for confusion to hide. The answer has to be a more intentional control layer, a way for business owners to see, organize, protect, and operate with confidence.

Whether a business uses Aetis or builds its own internal version of that discipline, the principle remains the same. Trust has to be designed. Security has to be built in. Accountability has to be visible. The operating layer has to serve the human promise, not swallow it.

That is the future I believe serious businesses must prepare for.

Trust is the advantage speed cannot fake

There will be companies that move fast and lose trust. There will be companies that move slowly and still lose trust because they are disorganized, unclear, or outdated. The strongest companies will learn to do something harder: move faster while becoming more trustworthy.

That is not a slogan. It is a discipline.

It means reviewing systems before they touch customers. It means protecting data before there is a crisis. It means explaining AI use before people become suspicious. It means training employees before mistakes become habits. It means measuring outcomes, not just activity. It means making sure the business can explain important decisions even when those decisions are supported by machines.

The world will reward speed. There is no question about that. But speed without trust will become fragile. It will win attention and lose loyalty. It will create activity and invite doubt. It will impress people at first and exhaust them later.

Trust is different. Trust compounds. Trust makes customers return. Trust makes teams more willing to change. Trust makes partners more willing to commit. Trust gives innovation a place to stand.

In a machine-speed world, the businesses that win will not be the ones that merely automate more. They will be the ones that make people feel safer, clearer, and more confident while everything else accelerates.

That is what Chapter 25 is really about. Not just the future of business, but the kind of business worth building for that future.

Part Five - The Future

Chapter 25

The Business Worth Building

The future will belong to businesses that remember why they exist.

That may sound simple, but it is one of the easiest things to forget in a fast world. When technology gets louder, leaders can become obsessed with the tool. When competitors move quickly, businesses can become obsessed with speed. When AI starts producing more content, more reports, more answers, and more options, people can start believing that the point of business is to keep up with the machine.

It is not.

The point of business is still to serve people, solve real problems, create value, earn trust, protect what matters, and build something that can stand when the noise changes. AI does not erase that. It exposes whether the business was built on that foundation in the first place.

That is why this final chapter matters. We have talked about speed. We have talked about systems. We have talked about cybersecurity, data, automation, leadership, customer trust, and the hidden war happening inside modern business. But underneath all of that is one question every owner, founder, executive, and team leader has to answer: what kind of business are you actually building?

Because AI can help you build almost anything faster. It cannot decide for you whether that thing is worth building.

The machine can accelerate the mission

AI is not the mission. It is an accelerant. That means it makes the mission move faster, but it does not give the mission meaning. If the mission is clear, AI can help it travel farther. If the mission is messy, AI can spread that mess more efficiently. If the mission is shallow, AI can make it louder without making it deeper.

This is why leadership matters so much in the AI era. A tool cannot replace the moral center of a company. A workflow cannot replace values. A dashboard cannot replace wisdom. A model cannot tell you what kind of reputation you want to earn, what kind of promises you are willing to make, what kind of customer you want to serve, or what kind of standard you refuse to lower.

A strong business uses AI to serve the mission. A weak business lets AI become the mission.

There is a big difference.

When AI serves the mission, it helps the business become clearer, faster, safer, and more useful. It removes needless friction. It helps people find information. It supports better decisions. It catches what humans might miss. It gives leaders more visibility. It helps the team spend less time chasing scattered details and more time doing meaningful work.

When AI becomes the mission, the business starts chasing novelty. It buys tools because they are impressive. It automates processes before it understands them. It measures output instead of impact. It starts sounding futuristic while quietly becoming less human.

The business worth building does not worship technology. It uses technology with discipline.

Do not build a faster version of a broken business

One of the most honest things a leader can admit is this: not every part of the business deserves to be automated yet.

Some processes should not be accelerated. They should be fixed. Some approvals should not be bypassed. They should be clarified. Some customer experiences should not be handed to a bot. They should be redesigned. Some data should not be dumped into a new system. It should be cleaned, protected, and understood first.

AI rewards readiness. It does not create readiness by magic.

This is where many businesses will stumble. They will take old confusion and wrap it in new technology. They will take scattered files, unclear roles, weak permissions, inconsistent customer service, and messy financial habits, then ask AI to make everything feel modern. For a little while, it might work on the surface. The business may look faster. It may sound more polished. It may produce more.

But eventually, the old disorder will show up again. It will show up in a wrong answer, a missed handoff, a customer who feels forgotten, an employee who does not know which instruction to trust, a report that no one can explain, or a security problem that should have been prevented.

A faster broken system is still broken. It is just harder to catch.

The business worth building is not the one that rushes to automate everything. It is the one that has the courage to ask, what needs to be made worthy of automation first?

That question separates serious builders from trend chasers.

Build for the person on the other side

The best businesses remember the person on the other side of the system. The customer filling out the form. The employee trying to understand the new process. The partner reviewing the proposal. The vendor waiting for a clear answer. The founder trying to make a responsible decision with imperfect information.

AI can make business feel less personal if leaders allow the system to become the relationship. But AI can also make business more personal when it helps the company remember details, reduce delays, honor context, and respond with greater care.

The difference is intention.

A business can use AI to blast more messages at more people, or it can use AI to understand what people actually need. It can use AI to replace listening, or it can use AI to make listening more organized. It can use AI to pressure customers into faster decisions, or it can use AI to make choices clearer and safer.

Every tool carries the values of the person using it.

That is why the human standard cannot disappear. People still need to feel seen. They need to feel respected. They need to know when a real person is responsible. They need to know that the company is not hiding behind automation when something important is at stake.

The business worth building uses AI to remove distance, not create it. It uses speed to serve people better, not rush them past their own good judgment. It uses intelligence to make the experience clearer, not manipulate trust.

Because at the end of every workflow, there is a person deciding whether your business feels safe enough to believe.

The new luxury is clarity

In the old business world, luxury often meant more: more features, more departments, more options, more pages, more meetings, more reports. In the AI era, the new luxury is clarity.

People are overwhelmed. They are surrounded by notifications, apps, offers, claims, advice, warnings, and decisions. They do not need every business to add more noise. They need businesses that make things easier to understand.

Clear pricing. Clear promises. Clear next steps. Clear ownership. Clear data practices. Clear boundaries around AI. Clear communication when something goes wrong. Clear evidence that the business knows what it is doing.

That kind of clarity is not accidental. It comes from internal discipline. A business cannot create clear customer experiences if the inside of the business is confused. It cannot give clear answers if the team does not share one source of truth. It cannot make clear promises if leadership has not defined what the company will and will not do.

AI can help produce clarity, but it cannot substitute for it. A generated summary is only useful if the underlying information is real. An automated message is only helpful if the process behind it is sound. A dashboard is only powerful if the data deserves to be trusted.

This is why the future will favor businesses that simplify without becoming shallow. The companies that win will not necessarily be the ones with the most complex technology. They will be the ones that use technology to make complexity easier for people to navigate.

In a world full of machine-speed noise, clarity will feel like care.

Small businesses are not out of the game

One of the fears I hear underneath many conversations about AI is that small businesses will not be able to compete. People look at large companies with massive budgets, large teams, and endless technology stacks, and they wonder if the game is already over.

It is not over.

The game is changing, but small businesses are not powerless. In many ways, they have advantages large companies struggle to keep. They can be closer to the customer. They can make decisions faster. They can change direction without moving an entire bureaucracy. They can build trust through direct relationships. They can adopt discipline without waiting for five committees to approve common sense.

AI gives small businesses leverage, but leverage has to be handled wisely. It can help a small team look more professional, respond more consistently, organize information better, protect operations, and make smarter decisions. But the advantage is not simply using AI. The advantage is using AI with focus.

A small business does not need every tool. It needs the right operating layer for its stage. It needs a clear way to manage customers, money, data, work, risk, and communication. It needs to know what matters most and what must never be compromised. It needs to move faster without becoming careless.

That is good news. Because small businesses do not win by copying giants. They win by becoming sharper, more trusted, and more disciplined versions of themselves.

The future will not only belong to the biggest companies. It will belong to the clearest companies. The most trusted companies. The companies that know how to use intelligence without losing identity.

Your authority comes from what you protect

In a noisy market, authority is often misunderstood. Some people think authority is about sounding impressive. Others think it is about having the biggest audience, the newest tools, or the loudest opinion. But real authority is quieter than that.

Real authority comes from responsibility.

It comes from knowing what you protect. You protect your customers from confusion. You protect your team from chaos. You protect your data from misuse. You protect your reputation from shortcuts. You protect your decisions from panic. You protect your mission from trends that do not belong to it.

That kind of authority does not require you to be cold or complicated. It does not require you to sound like a machine. In fact, the more technical the world becomes, the more valuable plainspoken leadership becomes. People need leaders who can translate complexity into usable truth. They need someone who can say, here is what matters, here is what does not, here is where we are going, and here is how we are going to do this responsibly.

That is the kind of authority this book is meant to build.

Not fake authority. Not fear-based authority. Not authority that depends on jargon. The kind that comes from seeing the invisible war clearly and helping other people navigate it.

Aetis and the larger promise

This is also the larger promise behind Aetis. Not simply software. Not simply cybersecurity. Not simply AI. The deeper idea is that modern business needs a secure control layer that helps people operate with more confidence, more visibility, and more discipline.

A business owner should not have to stitch together a dozen disconnected tools and hope the important things are protected. A team should not have to guess where the truth lives. A customer should not have to wonder whether speed is coming at the cost of safety. A leader should not have to choose between being modern and being responsible.

The future needs businesses that can do both.

That is why the work matters. The platform matters because the problem is real. The book matters because the conversation is urgent. The speaking matters because business owners need language for what they are already feeling. They know the world is changing. They know the tools are moving faster than the habits. They know trust is becoming harder to earn and easier to lose.

This book gives them a way to see it. Aetis gives them a way to respond to it. And your leadership gives them permission to believe they do not have to be technical to be serious about the future.

That is powerful.

The business worth building is brave enough to be human

The business worth building is not perfect. No business is. It will still make mistakes. It will still have hard days. It will still face uncertainty, competition, pressure, and change. AI will not remove those realities.

But the business worth building responds differently.

It does not hide from change. It learns. It does not worship speed. It directs it. It does not pretend technology is harmless. It governs it. It does not treat trust as decoration. It builds trust into the work. It does not ask humans to compete with machines at being machines. It asks humans to lead with judgment, courage, creativity, empathy, and responsibility.

That is the future I believe in. A future where business owners are not intimidated by AI, but also not careless with it. A future where small businesses have the confidence to modernize without losing their soul. A future where technology serves the mission instead of swallowing it. A future where security, clarity, and trust become everyday business standards, not luxuries reserved for giant corporations.

The invisible war is not just a battle against cyber threats, scattered tools, bad data, rushed decisions, and machine-speed pressure. It is also a battle for the kind of business world we want to create next.

We can build companies that are faster and emptier. Or we can build companies that are faster, safer, clearer, and more human.

That choice is still ours.

A closing word to the builder

If you are reading this as a business owner, founder, executive, operator, or dreamer, I want you to hear this clearly: you are not behind because you do not know every tool. You are not disqualified because you are still learning. You are not less capable because the technology feels bigger than your current systems.

The goal is not to know everything. The goal is to lead with enough clarity to build wisely.

Start where you are. Clean the data you depend on. Protect the information people trust you with. Decide what AI is allowed to do and what must stay human. Build the business brain. Create the operating rhythm. Train the team. Review the systems. Listen to the customer. Keep the promise.

You do not have to become less human to succeed in the AI era. You have to become more intentional.

That is the heart of this book. The AI era is not asking you to disappear into technology. It is asking you to build with more discipline, more courage, and more honesty than ever before.

The future will be fast. It will be intelligent. It will be competitive. It will be noisy. But it will still need people who know what they are building and why it matters.

Build that kind of business.

Build the business worth trusting.

Build the business worth protecting.

Build the business worth building.

www.ingramcontent.com/pod-product-compliance
Lightning Source LLC
LaVergne TN
LVHW091526200926
848483LV00002B/319